# MODELS AND ANALOGIES IN SCIENCE

# MODELS AND ANALOGIES
# IN SCIENCE

by Mary B. Hesse

UNIVERSITY OF NOTRE DAME PRESS

# Contents

# Introduction

If a scientific theory is to give an "explanation" of experimental data, is it necessary for the theory to be understood in terms of some model or some analogy with events or objects already familiar? Does "explanation" imply an account of the new and unfamiliar in terms of the familiar and intelligible, or does it involve only a correlation of data according to some other criteria, such as mathematical economy or elegance?

Questions of this sort have forced themselves upon scientists and philosophers at various stages of the development of scientific theory, and particularly since the latter half of the nineteenth century, when physicists found themselves obliged to abandon the search for mechanical models of the ether as explanations of the phenomena of light and electromagnetism. In 1914, in his book *La Théorie physique,* the French physicist and philosopher Pierre Duhem contrasted two kinds of scientific mind, in which he also saw a contrast between the Continental and English temperaments: on the one hand, the abstract, logical, systematizing, geometric mind typical of Continental physicists, on the other, the visualizing, imaginative, incoherent mind typical of the English—in Pascal's words, the "strong and narrow" against the "broad and weak." Correspondingly,

1

Duhem distinguished two kinds of theory in physics; the abstract and systematic on the one hand, and on the other, theories using familiar mechanical models. He explains the distinction in terms of electrostatics:

> This whole theory of electrostatics constitutes a group of abstract ideas and general propositions, formulated in the clear and precise language of geometry and algebra, and connected with one another by the rules of strict logic. This whole fully satisfies the reason for a French physicist and his taste for clarity, simplicity and order. . . .
>
> Here is a book [by Oliver Lodge] intended to expound the modern theories of electricity and to expound a new theory. In it are nothing but strings which move around pulleys, which roll around drums, which go through pearl beads . . . toothed wheels which are geared to one another and engage hooks. We thought we were entering the tranquil and neatly ordered abode of reason, but we find ourselves in a factory.[1]

Duhem admits that such models drawn from familiar mechanical gadgets may be useful psychological aids in suggesting theories, although, he thinks, this happens less often than is generally supposed. But this admission implies nothing about the truth or significance of the models, for many things may

1. *La Théorie physique,* ch. 4, 5.

be psychological aids to discovery, including astrological beliefs,  dreams, or even tea leaves, without implying that they are of any permanent significance in relation to scientific theory. Duhem's main objection to mechanical models is that they are incoherent and superficial and tend to distract the mind from the search for logical order. He is not much concerned, as other writers have been, with the possibility that models may mislead by being taken too literally as explanations of the phenomena, and so he does not object to fundamental mechanical theories, such as that of Descartes, where the attempt is made to reduce all phenomena to a few mechanical principles in a systematic way. But for Duhem the essence of such a theory lies not so much in its analogies with familiar mechanical objects and processes, but rather in its economic and systematic character. The ideal physical theory would be a mathematical system with deductive structure similar to Euclid's, unencumbered by extraneous analogies or imaginative representations.

These and similar views were directly challenged by the English physicist N. R. Campbell, in his book *Physics, the Elements,* published in 1920. A footnote in which Campbell refers to national tendencies to prefer mechanical or mathematical theory suggests that he has Duhem among others in mind in mounting his attack, although he does not mention Duhem by name. Campbell's main target is the view that models are *mere* aids to theory-construction, which can be thrown away when the theory has been developed, and his attack is based on two main arguments. *First,* he considers that we require to be intellectually satisfied by a theory if it is to be an explanation of phenomena, and this satisfaction implies that the theory has an intelligible interpretation in terms of a model, as well as having mere mathematical intelligibility and perhaps the formal characteristics of simplicity and economy. The *second* and more telling argument presupposes the *dynamic* character of theories. A theory in its scientific context is not a static museum piece, but is always being extended and modified to account for new phenomena. Campbell shows in terms of the development of the kinetic theory of gases how the billiard-ball model of this theory played an essential part in its extension, and he argues perceptively that, without the analogy with a model, any such extensions will be merely arbitrary. Moreover, without a model, it will be impossible to use a theory for one of the essential purposes we demand of it, namely to make predictions in new domains of phenomena. So he concludes:

> . . . analogies are not "aids" to the establishment of theories; they are an utterly essential part of theories, without which theories would be completely valueless and unworthy of the name. It is often suggested that the analogy leads to the formulation of the theory, but that once the theory is formulated the analogy has served its purpose and may be removed or forgotten. Such a sug-

gestion is absolutely false and perniciously misleading.[2]

Enough has been said to indicate the general tenor of the debate. The actual standpoints of Duhem and Campbell are affected by the state of their own contemporary physics, and there is no need to insist on the details of their arguments. Some of these certainly cannot survive actual evidence of the workability of new kinds of theory in modern physics, and in particular the restriction of the discussion to *mechanical* models (of which Duhem is more guilty than Campbell) requires to be modified. But many physicists would now hold in essentials with Duhem and would claim that Campbell's position has been decisively refuted by the absence of intelligible models in quantum physics; indeed, many would claim that something like Duhem's position must necessarily be the accepted philosophy underlying modern physical theory.

This essay has been written in the conviction that the debate has not been so decisively closed, and that an element of truth remains in Campbell's insistence that without models theories cannot fulfil all the functions traditionally required of them, and in particular that they cannot be genuinely predictive. The chapter which follows has been cast in the form of a debate between modern disciples of Duhem and Campbell, respectively. The protagonists finally

2. *Physics, the Elements,* p. 129.

agree, fairly amicably, to differ, but during the course of the argument they have, I think, succeeded in clarifying and settling some of the issues which often befog this topic. The Campbellian has also made some sort of a case for greater attention to be paid in the philosophy of science to logical questions about the nature and validity of analogical argument from models. The subsequent chapters attempt to pursue some of these logical questions, albeit in a preliminary and elementary fashion.

I should like to express my grateful thanks to Professor R. B. Braithwaite and Mr. G. Buchdahl for discussions which have inspired some of the points made here, although probably neither of them will recognize the arguments put into the mouths of my disputants as being positions which they would ever have defended. To avoid a great bulk of footnotes, I have collected in the suggestions for further reading most of the references to published work that I have found valuable in thinking about models and the logic of analogy.

# The Function of Models:
# A Dialogue

*Campbellian:* I imagine that along with most contemporary philosophers of science, you would wish to say that the use of models or analogues is not essential to scientific theorizing and that theoretical explanation can be described in terms of a purely formal deductive system, some of whose consequences can be interpreted into observables, and hence empirically tested, but that the theory as a whole does not require to be interpreted by means of any model.

*Duhemist:* Yes. I do not deny of course that models may be useful guides in suggesting theories, but I do not think they are essential, even as psychological aids, and they are certainly not *logically* essential for a theory to be accepted as scientific. When we have found an acceptable theory, any model that may have led us to it can be thrown away. Kekulé is said to have arrived at the structure of the benzene ring after dreaming of a snake with its tail in its mouth, but no account of the snake appears in the textbooks of organic chemistry.

*Campbellian:* I, on the other hand, want to argue that models in some sense *are* essential to the logic of scientific theories. But first let us agree on the sense in which we are using the word "model" when

7

we assert or deny that models are essential. I should like to explain my sense of the word by taking Campbell's well-worn example of the dynamical theory of gases. When we take a collection of billiard balls in random motion as a model for a gas, we are not asserting that billiard balls are in all respects like gas particles, for billiard balls are red or white, and hard and shiny, and we are not intending to suggest that gas molecules have these properties. We are in fact saying that gas molecules are *analogous* to billiard balls, and the relation of analogy means that there are some properties of billiard balls which are not found in molecules. Let us call those properties we know belong to billiard balls and not to molecules the *negative analogy* of the model. Motion and impact, on the other hand, are just the properties of billiard balls that we do want to ascribe to molecules in our model, and these we can call the *positive analogy*. Now the important thing about this kind of model-thinking in science is that there will generally be some properties of the model about which we do not yet know whether they are positive or negative analogies; these are the interesting properties, because, as I shall argue, they allow us to make new predictions. Let us call this third set of properties the *neutral analogy*. If gases are really like collections of billiard balls, except in regard to the known negative analogy, then from our knowledge of the mechanics of billiard balls we may be able to make new predictions about the expected behavior of gases. Of course the predictions may be wrong, but then we shall be led to conclude that we have the wrong model.

*Duhemist:* Your terminology of positive, negative, and neutral analogies is useful but is there not still a possible ambiguity about the sense of "model"? You have mentioned gas molecules and billiard balls. When you speak of the model for gases, do you mean the billiard balls, positive and negative analogy and all, or do you mean what we imagine when we try to picture gas molecules as ghostly little objects having some but not all the properties of billiard balls? I should say that both senses are widely used (among many others), but it is important to distinguish them.

*Campbellian:* I agree they should be distinguished, and I think we can do so conveniently by means of my terminology. Let us agree that when we speak of a model in its primary sense (in this discussion let us call it model₁), we are not speaking of another object which can, as it were, be built or imagined alongside the phenomena we are investigating. The model₁ is the imperfect copy (the billiard balls) *minus the known negative analogy,* so that we are only considering the known positive analogy, and the (probably open) class of properties about which it is not yet known whether they are positive or negative analogies. When we consider a theory based on a model as an explanation for a set of phenomena, we are considering the positive and neutral analogies, not the negative analogy, which we already know we can discard.

*Duhemist:* Are you not confusing "model" with the theory itself? There is no difference between the theory and the model$_1$ as you now explain it, so why use the word "model" at all?

*Campbellian:* Partly because there is a tendency, particularly among people of your school of thought, to use the word "theory" to cover only what I would call the known positive analogy, neglecting the features of the model which are its growing points, namely its neutral analogy. My whole argument is going to depend on these features, and so I want to make it clear that I am not dealing with static and formalized theories, corresponding only to the known positive analogy, but with theories in the process of growth. Also, since you disagree with me that models are essential to theories, you will necessarily use the word "theory" in a wider sense than my "model"—to cover formal deductive systems which have only a partial interpretation into observables. My models$_1$, on the other hand, are total interpretations of a deductive system depending on the positive and neutral analogies with the "copy."

Since I shall also want to talk about the second object or copy that includes the negative analogy, let us agree as a shorthand expression to call this "model$_2$." If it is indifferent which sense is meant, I shall simply use "model."

Let us now try to produce a reconstruction of the

use of models and analogies in a familiar example
—the wave models for sound and for light. At an
elementary level we can set up the following correspondences:

| WATER WAVES | SOUND | LIGHT |
| --- | --- | --- |
| Produced by mo-tion of water par-ticles | Produced by mo-tion of gongs, strings, etc. | Produced by mov-ing flame, etc. |
| Properties of re-flection | Echoes, etc. | Reflection in mir-rors, etc. |
| Properties of dif-fraction | Hearing round corners | Diffraction through small slits, etc. |
| Amplitude | Loudness | Brightness |
| Frequency | Pitch | Color |
| Medium: Water | Medium: Air | Medium: "Ether" |

The first three rows indicate some respects in
which these three processes appear to be alike to
fairly superficial observation. They are, for example,
the kind of properties that would go in Bacon's
Tables of Presence, or Mill's Agreements. In all
three cases there are present motion, something
transmitted indirectly from one place to another by
hitting an obstacle, and a bending round obstacles.
This suggests that the three processes are perhaps
alike in more fundamental respects, and in order to
investigate this possibility, we look more closely at
the one of the three about which we know most,
namely, water waves. We postulate, with Huygens,
that a disturbance of one particle communicates

itself to neighboring particles in such a way that ripples spread from the center of disturbance in concentric circles, and by means of the elementary mathematics of simple harmonic motion we are able to represent the amplitude and frequency of the waves and to derive the laws of reflection and diffraction. We have then a theory of water ripples consisting of equations of the type

$$y = a \sin 2\pi f x$$

where $y$ is the height of the water at the point $x$ measured horizontally, $a$ is the maximum height or amplitude of the ripples, and $f$ is their frequency. From this mathematical theory some laws of the process, such as the equality of the angles of incidence and reflection, can be deduced.

So far we have two sources of information to aid our construction of theories for sound and for light, namely, their observed properties and their observed analogies with water waves, and it is important to notice that both of them appeal only to descriptions of "observable" events. We may define *observation statements* as those descriptive statements whose truth or falsity in the face of given empirical circumstances would be agreed upon by all users of English with or without scientific training. Let us also introduce the term *explicandum* for the set of observation statements connected with the phenomena we are attempting to explain by means of a theory—that is, in this case, the observed properties of sound or of light. All users of English might not, of course, *notice* the analogies between the three processes until they are pointed out, and up to this point they may have no more significance than the fact that the class of fingers on a hand and petals on a buttercup are similar in that both have five members. But when the analogies have been pointed out, no esoteric insight and no specifically scientific knowledge are required to recognize that they exist. It is not quite the same with the mathematical theory of water waves, for here some knowledge of trigonometry is required, but there is no difficulty in understanding the *terms* "height of water," "frequency of waves," etc. into which the mathematical symbols are interpreted. In this sense the mathematical system is "about" (has its interpretation in terms of) observable events.

Now consider what happens when we make use of the known theory of water waves and the analogies between them and sound in order to construct a theory of sound. The analogies suggest that sound is produced by the motion of air particles propagated in concentric spherical waves from a center of disturbance. Since we know that the greater the disturbance of water the greater the amplitude of the waves, and the greater the disturbance of gongs, strings, hammers, etc., the greater the noise produced, it is easy to identify loudness of sound with amplitude of sound waves, and, similarly, experiences with strings of varying lengths persuade us that pitch or sound is to be identified with frequency of sound waves. In some such way we construct one-to-one correspondences between the observable properties of sound (the explicandum) and those of water waves (the model$_2$), and we are then in a position to test the mathematical wave theory as a theory of sound. Further tests of this kind, of course, may or may not show the theory to be satisfactory. I am not claiming that the use of analogy leads us to an infallible theory, only that it is used in this way to *suggest* a theory. I do not suppose you will want to dispute this so far.

*Duhemist:* No, I have no objection to your reconstruction of the way this particular model might be used. But I am unhappy about the sense in which you say that the initial analogies and the interpretations of the mathematical wave theory in terms of water can be said to be "observable," as contrasted, I suppose, with the air particles which are not observable. I cannot see that there is an important difference here. Surely, to "observe" a similarity between the behavior of ripples at the edge of the swimming bath and the behavior of sound in a mountain valley is a far from superficial observation. It requires a very sophisticated framework of physical ideas in which, for example, the phenomena of echoes are described in terms of a train of physical causes initiated by a shout, rather than in terms of an imitative spirit of the mountains.

*Campbellian:* Yes, I agree with this, and your example indicates that, contrary to what some empiricist philosophers seem to have held, "observation-descriptions" are not written on the face of events to be transferred directly into language but are already "interpretations" of events, and the kind of interpretation depends on the framework of assumptions of a language community. It can plausibly be argued that there is *no* descriptive statement, not even the "blue-here-now" beloved of sense-data theorists, which does not go beyond what is "given" in the act of observing. But I do not wish to pursue this argument here. Would you be prepared to agree that scientific theories bring something *new* into our descriptions of events, and that it is therefore possible to make a distinction between the observation statements of a given language community sharing a framework of assumptions, and the statements going beyond this shared framework which are introduced in scientific theories? It is in contrast with these novelties, which may be called *theoretical statements,* containing *theoretical terms,* that certain at present agreed kinds of description may be called observable. This is to make the distinction a pragmatic one, relative to the assumptions of a given language community, but it does not mean that the traditional empiricist problem of the relation between theory and observation disappears. To realize that every hen was once a chicken is not to absolve oneself from the task of finding out how a hen gives birth to a chicken.

*Duhemist:* Our dispute does not turn on the precise nature of the observation language, and I will accept your pragmatic description of it. But I have another objection to your account of the genesis of a theory of sound. You seem to imply that there are two sorts of theory-construction going on here. First there is the theory of water waves, which is arrived at by making a hypothesis about the propagation of disturbances, expressing this in mathematical language, and deducing from it the observed properties of water waves. There is no mention of any analogies or models here. But in the case of sound it is said that one-to-one correspondences between properties of water and properties of sound are set up first, and then the mathematical wave theory is transferred to sound. This may well be the way in which theories are often arrived at in practice, but you have said nothing to show that reference to the water model is essential or that there is any difference in principle between the relations of theory and observation in the two cases. Both theories consist of a deductive system together with an interpretation of the terms occurring in it into observables, and from both systems can be deduced relations which, when so interpreted, correspond to observed relations, such as the law of reflection. This is all that is required of an explanatory theory. You have implicitly acknowledged it to be sufficient in the case of water waves, and it is also sufficient in the case of sound waves. If we had never heard of water waves, we should still be able to use the same information about sound to obtain the same result. The information consists of the observed production of sound by certain motions of solid bodies, the relations between the magnitudes of these motions and the loudness of the sound, and between lengths of strings and pitch of note, and the phenomena of echoes and bending.

All of these can be deduced from a mathematical wave theory with appropriate interpretation, without mentioning the water-wave model, and, what is more important, without supposing that there is anything connected with the transmission of sound or light which is analogous to water—that is, without supposing there are some "hidden" motions of particles having the same relation to these observed properties of sound or light that the motions of water particles have to the properties of water waves. In fact, it would be very misleading to suppose any such thing, because some of the further consequences derived from a theory of water waves turn out *not* to be true if transferred, by the one-to-one correspondence, to sound and light transmission.

*Campbellian:* No, but the reason for this in the case of sound at least is not that there is *no* wave model but that ripples are the *wrong* wave model. The oscillation of particles constituting sound waves takes place along the direction of transmission of the sound, like the motion of a piston, and not at right angles to that direction, as with ripples. But what I have just described is itself a model of the motions of air particles derived by analogy with observable events such as the action of buffers on the trucks of a train or (to take Huygens' example) the transmission of pressure along a line of billiard balls when the ball at one end is struck in the direction of the line, and the ball at the other end moves off by itself in the same direction.

*Duhemist:* I did not intend to say that in many cases an alternative model cannot be found when the first breaks down, but only that mention of a model is not part of the logical structure of an explanatory theory, and that it is not even always a useful device for finding such a theory, for it may positively suggest the wrong theory.

It is a question of logic I should like your reactions to. I am impressed, you see, by the situation throughout a large part of modern physics, where it is impossible to find any model like the model of air motions for sound, and where nevertheless the criteria for a deductive theory which I have outlined are still satisfied, and theory construction and testing go on much as before. It may be less satisfactory to the imagination to have no picturable model, and more difficult to construct theories without it, but the continuance of physics in the same logical shape as before shows that the model is not logically necessary to the process.

*Campbellian:* I am not convinced that there is

such an absence of models in modern physics as you suggest, and I may come back to that later. Also, it is a little misleading to speak of "pictures" as if they were synonymous with models, for I would say, for example, that a three-dimensional space curved in a fourth dimension is a perfectly good *model* in relativity theory, but it is certainly not *picturable*. A model, for me, is any system, whether buildable, picturable, imaginable, or none of these, which has the characteristic of making a theory *predictive* in a sense I shall describe later when I try to substantiate my claim that models are logically essential for theories.

But let us stick for the moment to our simple example, because it is easier to bring out the difference between us there. If I understand you, you are saying that in the case of sound waves there is no point even in speaking about motions of air particles, because these are not part of the observed data you list, and we can explain these data equally well by means of a mathematical theory, *some* of whose consequences can be interpreted to give relations between the observables. You will at least admit that here there is a difference between the two theories I described, those for ripples and for sound, in that the motions of water particles *are* observable in the pragmatic sense we have agreed on, and so all the symbols in the equations of the ripple theory are interpretable as observables. In the case of sound, however, we cannot "observe" in this sense the amplitude and frequency of the waves, indeed we cannot observe "waves" at all, we can only infer them from data such as impact of hammer on gong, and vibration of strings. Do you wish to say that a theory of sound need not mention "waves" at all, since these are not observable?

*Duhemist:* I am not suggesting that convenient and universal modes of speech such as this should necessarily be dropped, but let us see what exactly we mean by talking about sound waves. We do not mean just the same as we do when talking about water waves, because, as we have seen, sound waves are longitudinal and not transverse. The word persists because both theories use the same mathematical formalism, which we call the wave equation, differently applied in the two cases. What ripples and sound waves have in common is completely contained in the mathematical formalism, and it is this we point to by continuing to use the word "wave." Of course, I am not denying that it is legitimate to think of the propagation of sound in terms of pulsating spheres of air particles, so long as what we mean by this is controlled by what we know from observation about sound, and not by reference to some *other* process. I suppose this can be expressed in your terminology by saying that if the positive analogy between sound and a model of pulsating spheres is believed to be complete, then this model is identical with our theory of sound, and there is no harm in using the language of the model$_1$ as an interpretation of the mathematics of the theory. But I am denying that we can always get this sort of model, and that when we can't we somehow have less of an explanation.

*Campbellian:* I am surprised you are prepared to allow as much as this for common modes of speech, and I am not sure you are consistent in doing so. If you had regarded all talk of "oscillations of air particles" as misleading and dispensable, I should have respected your consistency, but I should then have attacked you on the grounds that you do not give a plausible account of the meaning of theoretical terms. On what I take to be the consistent formalist view, the theory in this case consists *only* of a formal deductive system—marks on paper manipulated according to certain rules—together with the interpretations in terms of observables, so that the only meaning that can be given to, for instance, the parameter $a$ in the wave equation is in terms of intensity of sound at the point where that is recorded. There is nothing to say about $a$ during the time which elapses between the banging of the gong and the reception of the sound at some distant point. I can say, on the other hand, that $a$ has an interpretation at all times during the passage of the sound—namely, it is the amplitude of oscillations of air particles, even though these are "unobservable." Thus I have a solution to the so-called problem of the "meaning of theoretical terms."

*Duhemist:* Well, of course all kinds of definitions

of theoretical terms have been suggested to cover cases like this, and in the case of sound waves a conditional definition in terms of observables might be given in the form:

> For all $(x, y, t)$, the amplitude of a sound wave at $(x, y)$ is $a$ if a microphone placed at $(x, y)$ at time $t$ records sound of intensity proportional to $a^2$.

But it is not always possible to give definitions even of this conditional kind, and when it is not, I am content to say that the meaning of "amplitude of sound wave" is given indirectly by the position of $a$ in the deductive system, and the fact that some consequences of the system, when interpreted, have ordinary empirical meaning.

*Campbellian:* So when you spoke of "pulsating spheres of air particles," you were not smuggling in a reference to any model$_2$, but only intended these words to be a way of speaking about the mathematical symbols? According to you it would be wrong to look up their meaning in a dictionary on this occasion—what is required is to look up the position of the corresponding symbols in the deductive system. This is surely a very strange account of "meaning"? It implies that "indirect meaning" can be given to any word I like to coin by inserting it in a deductive system, for example in the syllogism:

All toves are white

My car is a tove
*therefore* My car is white,

the conclusion of which is observable. "Toves" now has indirect meaning in your sense.

*Duhemist:* This account of indirect meaning must be regarded as necessary but not sufficient. To make it sufficient I should have to add that for a theoretical term to have scientific meaning in this way, it must occur in a deductive system which is seriously considered in science, that is, one which has many observable consequences in different circumstances, all of which are confirmed by observation and none refuted. This is entirely a question for scientific research, an empirical, not a logical question, and so the conditions for a theoretical term to have scientific meaning cannot be logically formalized. But it is clear that your syllogism about toves would not qualify.

*Campbellian:* This still seems to me very strange, the more so because you have agreed to accept an account of observational and theoretical terms in which the distinction between them is not logical but pragmatic. If you accept this you must allow for the frontier between them to shift as science progresses. This is done in my account by saying that we *discover* that sound waves *are* pulsating spheres of air particles *in the ordinary sense of these words,* and if this is accepted by everybody in the language community (as I suppose it is in ours), it does not much matter where the line of "observability" is drawn. Admittedly it would be odd in ordinary speech to talk about "observing" air pulses, but a statement about them might well function as an observation statement in a particular scientific experiment, that is to say, everyone would accept its truth or falsity as the final court of appeal without deducing further "observable" consequences from it. On your account I do not see how "pulsating spheres of air particles" ever gets into ordinary language, because you have specifically denied that these words are used in their ordinary sense.

*Duhemist:* My account is not in the least inconsistent with what we have previously agreed—in fact, I have given an account of *how* the frontier of observability shifts while you have not. The essence of this shift is surely that ordinary language itself changes—when we talk about air pulses we are *not* using the words in exactly the sense they previously had, and what I have done is precisely to explain how ordinary language is extended to take in new senses of these words, depending on the structure of the scientific theory in which they occur. You, on the contrary, have not explained how the ordinary senses of words change. Moreover, I think you have smuggled in a quite different issue here, namely, the question of the "reality" of the air pulses. You seem to imply that I am committed to a nonrealistic view, to saying that they are fictional entities or heuristic devices or what-not, but this is not the case. For me, to say that "air pulses exist" means just what I have explained—they are entities referred to by (the values of variables in) a deductive system having all characteristics of an accepted scientific theory that I have described. I do hold that *models* are heuristic devices, but I am not committed to holding that theoretical entities understood wholly as interpretations of an accepted mathematical theory are also. If you like, my theoretical entities are related to your models in having the *known positive analogy only*.

*Campbellian:* You have certainly made your position clearer, and I agree that we need not differ on the subject of existence of theoretical entities. We differ on what it is that is asserted to exist. I say that to assert a theory is to assert a $model_1$, positive *and* neutral analogy; you say it is to assert the positive analogy only, and according to you the neutral analogy is merely a heuristic device.

*Duhemist:* Of course, the theory may not be describable in terms of models at all, in cases where I deny that there are models. Then in order to assert the existence of a theoretical entity, we must either coin new words or give old words a new significance by the method of indirect meaning in deductive systems I have described. To go back to your original examples, the word "ether," which you have put in quotes in the third column of your table, was surely a word adopted and given significance in just this way," that is to say, there were some theories seriously considered at one stage in physics in which the ether had a well-defined place in a deductive system and the observable consequences of its properties could be empirically tested.

*Campbellian:* I am not satisfied that this is sufficient. I want to say that the well-defined place it had was due to its being understood in terms of wave models and that its meaning was given by a series of analogies of the form:

$$\frac{\text{water waves}}{\text{water particles}} :: \frac{\text{sound waves}}{\text{air particles}} :: \frac{\text{light waves}}{\text{ether particles}}$$

*Duhemist:* I do not really understand how "meanings" are given by analogies in this way at all. Are you saying simply that *when* there is a model$_2$ for a theory, as in the case of this theory of light, then "air" and "ether" are interpretations of the same set of symbols in the theory, air in the case of sound and ether in the case of light? If so, I agree that we may acquire an intuitive understanding of "ether" in this indirect way, by analogy with the air model$_2$. But since I do not regard models as part of the logic of theories, I cannot regard this sense of "meaning" as interesting for the logician.

*Campbellian:* I do mean by my analogical relations what you suggest, but I also mean something more, which I hope to convince you *is* part of the logic of theories. Let us go back to the example and try to fill out my account of the way the theory of sound is arrived at. I am prepared to concede your objection that, given all the observational information I have allowed myself, I could have gone straight to a mathematical wave theory from which the observations could be deduced, without going through the process of finding one-to-one correspondences with water waves. There will generally be an indefinite number of such mathematical theories, but I agree with you that there is no guarantee that the water-wave model$_2$ will lead to the correct theory, so you rightly ask whether I can have any reasons for using this analogy except the comfortable feeling that I have seen the mathematics before. Well, I think I have a reason, and I can explain it by taking a slightly different situation.

Suppose we are now attempting to construct a theory of light. Your procedure will be to find, no matter how, a mathematical system from which the observed properties of the explicandum—say, reflection and refraction—can be deduced, and for this you will only demand interpretations of the formulae which yield the observable relations you wish to explain. Suppose, by whatever method or lack of method you use, you do choose the mathematical wave theory out of the indefinite number of possibilities. I shall arrive at the same theory by noticing the analogies between light and sound, and setting up a model$_1$ of light transmission in terms of oscillation of particles in a medium. Now, we must distinguish between the various results we can obtain. You will be able to deduce the simple laws of reflection and refraction by using space coordinate and intensity observables, but these will be the only terms in the theory which you will interpret as observables. So far you will have deduced geometrical optics from a mathematical wave theory. If you want to do more than this, you will have to interpret the symbol $f$ in your equation $y = a \sin 2\pi f x$, as well as the symbols $a$ and $x$.

Now you may have observational information that will allow you to do this directly. For example, you may derive from your theory equations relating to the passage of light through a prism, in which you notice that the angle of refraction depends on the value of $f$. If you also have experimental data on the production of a spectrum of colors by the prism, it will be reasonable to set up a one-to-one correspondence between values of $f$ and colors in the spectrum. The theory will then have shown itself capable of explaining the laws of dispersion as well as those of geometrical optics. But suppose you do not know the prism experiment or any other relating to colors. How is $f$ to be interpreted? You may of course make a guess, that since there are lights of different colors and there is an available parameter $f$ in the theory, it would be worth investigating whether the identification of values of $f$ with different colors will yield a correspondence between theory and experiment. Or you may decide that $f$ is uninterpretable; it is part of the machinery of the deductive theory but has no observable correlate. In this case you will not be able to include dispersion in your theory. Have I described your possible procedures correctly?

*Duhemist:* Yes, I will accept that in principle I should have these three possibilities in the case of a hitherto uninterpreted term in the theory. Of course the example you are using hardly brings out the points in a realistic way, because the wave equation was not introduced into optics until after the facts of color dispersion were already known, and so there was little difficulty about this particular identification. But I can see that in other cases there might be no obvious identification of a theoretical term; and then one might, as you suggest, decide to leave it uninterpreted, as in the case of a Schrödinger $\psi$-function in some schools of quantum physics; or one might make what you call a guess, but I should prefer to call a hypothesis, about its interpretation and investigate the experimental consequences of the hypothesis. What I cannot see is that you are any better off when it comes to interpreting a feature of your model. You will of course know that $f$ is what corresponds to the frequency of waves in the model, but in the absence of any observations connecting color with the laws of geometrical optics, which you have already explained by the theory, how does that help you to identify frequency of waves with color? You have the same choice that I have, either to leave $f$ uninterpreted, and hence "frequency of waves" uncorrelated with anything in your theory of light, or to resort to guesswork.

*Campbellian:* I used the word "guess" rather than "hypothesis" to bring out the fact that on your account of the nature of theories you *cannot give any reasons* for choosing to examine one interpretation rather than any other. And I notice that you did not give any actual example of a theoretical term being interpreted without the help of a model. It is no accident that it is difficult to think of an example, because I suggest there always in practice *are* reasons for examining a hypothetical interpretation, and these reasons are drawn from models.

*Duhemist:* Why should I give any reasons before having carried out experimental tests? I cannot give any reasons for choosing one theory rather than another until I have tested it, and the interpretation of a particular theoretical term is only an element in a theory, to be considered as part of the whole. But you have not answered my question about your own procedure. How does your model help you to give reasons for your interpretation?

*Campbellian:* This is where I appeal to the analogy between the model and the phenomena to be explained. Let us first see how I can interpret the parameter *a* of the theory, which is already correlated in my model with the amplitude of the waves. I suggest that the model$_2$ immediately makes it reasonable to suppose that "magnitude" of the waves corresponds with "magnitude" of the light, and in the case of light, "magnitude" means brightness. Just as a greater wave disturbance means a louder sound, so does a greater wave disturbance mean a brighter light, although this cannot be investigated directly since we cannot "make a greater wave disturbance" by moving a body as we can with sound. The hypothesis that this is the case comes from an analogy of the following kind:

$$\frac{\text{loudness}}{\text{properties of sound}} :: \frac{\text{brightness}}{\text{properties of light}}$$

I suggest that this analogy is found in the language before any wave theory is thought of. It is independent of the particular theory of light we are considering and so can be used to develop this theory.

*Duhemist:* One might, surely, just as plausibly suggest that brightness is correlated with shrillness, or loudness with purple or scarlet (called, be it noted, "loud" colors).

*Campbellian:* Admittedly there may be some ambiguities of this kind, but if we consider the points of similarity of loudness and brightness—the scale of intensities from absence of sound or light to indefinitely large degrees of it, the analogies between their effects on our sense organs ("deafening" and "blinding"), and so on, the suggested correspondence seems the most plausible.

*Dehumist:* All right, but what about the correspondence between pitch, frequency, and color which you must claim if your method is to work for interpreting the symbol $f$?

*Campbellian:* This is, admittedly, more difficult.

I do not, for example, see how the correspondence of frequency of waves with pitch could have been arrived at without observed correlations involving such things as vibrating strings. In the case of sound used as a model for light there is some plausibility in claiming a pre-scientific analogy:

$$\frac{\text{pitch}}{\text{properties of sound}} :: \frac{\text{color}}{\text{properties of light}}$$

if we think of the various metaphors from sound to light—Locke's blind man's "scarlet sound of trumpets," and the use of such terms as "harmony" and "clash," appealing to analogies of pleasure and pain in their effects on our sense organs.

*Duhemist:* I am not at all convinced that this roundabout way of recognizing analogies can be shown to be other than entirely arbitrary, but even if it can, you seem to me only to have given me one way of making my "guess" at an interpretation of a theoretical term. You have not shown that it constitutes any *reason* for expecting a guess made by this method to be a right or even fruitful one.

*Campbellian:* I hope you will waive for the moment the question of whether any objective analogies of the kind I describe actually exist, because I hope to go into this in more detail later. Meanwhile, I should like to examine the objection you have just made. There are two things I should like to say about it. First, I claim that to assert an analogy between amplitude of waves and loudness of sound or brightness of light, even before any experimental correlation is known, *is* to give a reason for the interpretation of the symbol *a* of a kind which can never be given on your account of the matter.

*Duhemist:* Let me interrupt you before you go any further. Of course, *if* it is possible to find a model$_2$, as it is in this case, an interpretation derived from the model$_2$ can be said to have the reason that it is derived from the model$_2$, and this distinguishes it from any interpretation I might decide to make. But this is pure evasion. I cannot accept a reason *in terms of* a model, for I claim that no model is required. I am asking for a reason for assuming that the model *is* required, or even that it is likely to lead to a better interpretation than one I may make.

*Campbellian:* Of course I cannot expect you to accept a reason appealing to a model, but what I want to point out is that as scientists use the word "reason" in this context, they *will* accept reasons appealing to models. This can be seen in the way they make predictions from models and use them as tests of theories. A prediction will be thought to be reasonable if it follows from an "obvious interpretation" given to a theoretical term by appeal to a model. If the prediction comes off, the theory and its model$_1$ will be regarded as strengthened, whereas if it fails to come off, this may be regarded as sufficiently serious to refute the theory and the model$_1$ together. For example, the corpuscular model of light was regarded as refuted when the obvious interpretation that two corpuscles falling on one spot would produce twice the intensity of light produced by one was shown to be contrary to diffraction experiments. That the model led to the wrong interpretation was in this instance a "reason" for abandoning the whole theory.

*Duhemist:* I am not clear why on your account it should be, for you have already allowed for the possibility that a model$_2$ may not correspond to the phenomena in *all* respects. Why cannot the feature which fails in this instance be removed to the negative analogy and the rest of the corpuscular model$_1$ retained?

*Campbellian:* To answer this would certainly require further analysis. Roughly, it would turn on the fact that some properties of models$_2$ are more "essential" than others, that is to say are causally more closely connected or tend to co-occur more frequently. For example, color is not an essential property of a billiard ball from the point of view of mechanics, but momentum is. If a prediction derived from color fails, this does not essentially affect a mechanical model$_1$, but if something derived from momentum fails, the model$_1$ is refuted.

*Duhemist:* But such refutation still depends on the assumption that a theory must have a model, which I am denying. And your example plays into my hands, for we know that the "essential property" you have appealed to in the case of the corpuscular theory of light is *not* now allowed to refute that theory. The quantum theory of radiation accommodates both diffraction experiments and model-talk about light particles. But the way particles and other models are used in quantum theory is quite consistent with my account. The theory is regarded as satisfactory if it is possible to deduce observed results from the mathematical formalism plus interpretation of some of its terms, and models$_2$ are used as only mnemonic and heuristic devices when convenient. In this theory models$_2$ need not even be consistent with one another to be useful.

*Campbellian:* I want to come back to this question of models in quantum theory later, but before that, let us look at this question of prediction more carefully, for this is my second point in answer to your challenge to me to produce reasons for using models.

I have suggested that my model enables me to make predictions because it leads to new and obvious interpretations of some theoretical terms which may then be used to derive new relations between observables. You reply that *any* assignment of a new interpretation, with or without the use of a model, will enable you to make predictions, and that there is no reason to have more confidence in my predictions than in yours. I agree that I have not yet given any reason, but I still want for a moment to pursue my point that the *kind of prediction required* can only be obtained by using models.

I take it that we both agree that a criterion for a

theory is that it should be falsifiable by empirical tests. Falsifiability is closely connected with predictive power, although they cannot quite be identified without further analysis. I want to point out that usage of the criterion of falsifiability covers at least three requirements on theories, only the strongest of which is sufficient to establish the superiority of my theory-plus-model over your formal theory. Let us consider three types of falsifiability and three corresponding types of theory, *G, A,* and *B.*

## Type G

In science a single observation statement hardly ever purports to describe only one unique event, but the set of events that would be observed under sufficiently similar circumstances at any time. Hence an observation statement may always be said to be falsifiable in the sense that the circumstances it describes, or sufficiently similar circumstances, may always, in principle, be repeated; hence it is conceivable that a statement which has been confirmed in the past may be falsified in the future. Questions about what would constitute "sufficiently similar circumstances," and what we should be disposed to say about an unexpected falsification of this kind need not detain us, because it is clear that such a sense of "falsifiable" is far too weak to satisfy those who wish to say that a condition for scientific theories is that they are falsifiable. A theory must do more than predict that the same observation statements that have been confirmed in the past will, in sufficiently similar circumstances, be confirmed in the future.

A scientific theory is required to be falsifiable in the sense that it leads to new observation statements which can be tested, that is, that it leads to new and perhaps unexpected and interesting predictions. But here there is an ambiguity. The weaker sense of such a requirement is that new correlations can be found between the *same* observation predicates; the stronger sense is that new correlations can also be found which involve new observation predicates. It will be convenient to introduce some notation here. I want to argue on the basis of your own account, because I think it does provide some *necessary* conditions that theories must satisfy; what I deny is that they are *sufficient*. Let us consider an observation language containing observation predicates $O_1, \ldots O_j, P_1, \ldots P_k$. Suppose there is a set of observation statements each of which is *accepted,* that is to say, each member of the set expresses an empirical correlation between some of the $O$'s and $P$'s which, at a given stage of use of the language, is accepted as true. If the set also exhausts all such accepted statements it will be called the *accepted* set. It represents then a science of these particular observables at the stage of empirical generalizations, before explanatory theories have been introduced. It may not, of course, exhaust *all* the true statements containing $O$'s and $P$'s, because there may be some correlations which remain unnoticed at this stage.

Now consider a set of theoretical predicates (the $T$'s) and a theory containing them which has as consequences all those observation statements of the accepted set which contain $O$'s and only $O$'s. That is to say, the theory is, in your sense, an explanation of the accepted statements containing only $O$'s. This theory may or may not, in addition, contain statements with observation predicates other than the $O$'s, namely the $P$'s. Falsifiability in senses $A$ and $B$ can now be explained as follows.

## Type A

Suppose the theory does *not* contain any $P$'s. Then it can have no consequences relating to predicates other than the $O$'s. Thus it cannot be used to explain the remaining statements of the accepted set containing any of the $P$'s, nor can it be used to predict correlations between them which are true but not yet accepted. That is to say, it is not falsifiable in the stronger sense. It may, however, be possible to use it to predict correlations between the $O$'s which are true but not yet accepted. Such a theory will be said to be *weakly falsifiable* or *weakly predictive* and will be called a *formal theory*. Many of the so-called "mathematical models" of modern cosmological, economic, and psychological theory are of this kind; they are mathematical hypotheses designed to fit experimental data, in which either there are no theoretical terms or if there are such terms, they are not further interpreted in a model$_2$.

## Type B

Suppose, however, the theory does contain some of the *P*'s. We may dismiss the case in which it contains them only in statements which contain no *T*'s, for then these statements cannot properly be said to be part of the theory, although they may be part of a scheme of empirical generalizations which remain wholly within the observation language. The theory may, however, contain some of the *P*'s in some statements which also contain some *T*'s. Such a theory may then yield as consequences observation statements containing any of these *P*'s, and hence may explain members of the accepted set containing them and may predict new correlations between them. It will then be said to be *strongly falsifiable* or *strongly predictive*.

Now consider how statements containing *T*'s and *P*'s (call them *P*-statements) could come to be introduced into the theory. They are not introduced by considering the observable relations between the *P*'s, because we have supposed that the theory was designed in the first place as an explanation of the *O*'s not the *P*'s. They are not introduced arbitrarily, because if they were there would be no reason why any particular statement should be introduced rather than any other, and such a theory could not be taken seriously as a predictive theory. Also, it would not, as a whole, be falsifiable, because falsification of one arbitrarily introduced *P*-statement could be dealt with by replacing it with another, leaving the rest of the theory unaffected. The only other possibility is that $P$-statements are introduced for reasons *internal to the theory*. These reasons, moreover, cannot be concerned merely with the formal properties of the theory—for example, its formal symmetry or simplicity—because they must be reasons for asserting particular things in the theoretical language about particular observation predicates (the $P$'s), and though the theoretical predicates may be seen from the formalist point of view as uninterpreted symbols, even from this point of view the observation predicates may not. Hence the set of $P$-statements must be interpreted in *terms of the theory*. It is this interpretation which, I maintain, is given by the model, and which requires the whole theory to have a model-interpretation.

*Duhemist:* I am not sure I have followed your symbolism. Surely the $P$'s are already interpreted, since they are observation predicates?

*Campbellian:* Yes, but I am concerned with how they get into the theory. By the conditions of my problem they are not introduced in virtue of their correlations with other observation predicates, hence they must have an interpretation in a model$_2$ which also provides an interpretation of the *theoretical* predicates. Consider my example of sound and light waves, where sound waves are a model$_2$ for the theory of light. Here the $O$'s might be position coordinates and intensities of light, and the $P$'s color predicates.

The theory of reflection and refraction explains the accepted $O$-statements but says nothing about the $P$'s. The question is, how do the $P$'s get into the theory to enable it to make predictions about color? They have to get in in the form of $P$-statements correlating the $P$'s with values of the parameter $f$, and $f$ is a *theoretical predicate*. Now the model$_2$ comes in as an interpretation of all the $T$'s into predicates referring to sound waves. $f$ is the frequency of sound waves, or pitch. This model$_2$, together with my suggested analogy "pitch corresponds to color," gives the interpretation "$f$ in the theory of light corresponds to color," and the theory now yields predictions about color. This can be represented schematically:

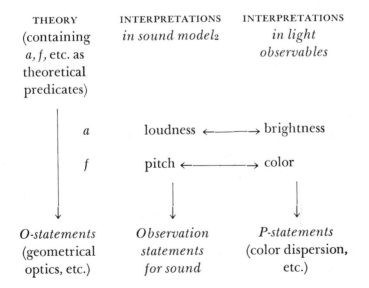

| THEORY (containing $a, f$, etc. as theoretical predicates) | INTERPRETATIONS *in sound model$_2$* | INTERPRETATIONS *in light observables* |
|---|---|---|
| $a$ | loudness ⟷ brightness | |
| $f$ | pitch ⟷ color | |
| $O$-statements (geometrical optics, etc.) | *Observation statements for sound* | $P$-statements (color dispersion, etc.) |

Here signs of equality indicate interpretations, within a theory, of theoretical predicates into observation predicates; double arrows indicate the direction of deduction; and double arrows indicate observable relations of analogy.

*Duhemist:* I can see that you are asking for a double interpretation of the $P$'s, once into observables and once into the model$_2$, and this is because you want to predict the observable $P$-statements by using the model$_2$.

But let me return to your argument in favor of the step involving the analogies between light and sound. I can see from your diagram that the analogies as well as the interpretations are of two kinds. The first kind are the one-to-one correspondences between theoretical predicates and predicates of the model$_2$, on the one hand, and between theoretical predicates and light observables on the other, giving one-to-one correspondences between predicates referring to light and to sound in virtue of the same formal theory. This, I take it, is the conventional use of "analogy" in mathematical physics, as when Kelvin exhibited analogies between fluid flow, heat flow, electric induction, electric current, and magnetic field, by showing that all are describable by the same equations with appropriate interpretations in each case. But you are asking for something in addition to this, namely, a sense of analogy in terms of which you can make these one-to-one correspondences *before you have got the theory,* by some kind of prescientific recognition of analogies such as pitch: color. Is this correct?

*Campbellian:* Certainly. My whole point is that it is necessary to have these correspondences before the theory, otherwise the theory is not predictive or falsifiable in the strong sense.

*Duhemist:* I think the weakest part of your argument is where you distinguish your senses *A* and *B* of falsifiability. Even if I admit for a moment that strong falsifiability is required, I cannot accept that *P*-statements can only be introduced into theories by means of your dubious analogies. There are other ways of extending theories which do not deserve your epithet "arbitrary." They give, of course, no guarantee of success, but neither does your model method.

*Campbellian:* If you think there are other methods which will do all that my models do, I think it is up to you to exhibit them. I have already said I do not think merely formal considerations of simplicity and so on are sufficient, because they do not by themselves supply an *interpretation* of the theory as extended, and hence do not supply predictions in a new field of observables. If "simplicity" were extended to apply also to interpretation, then I think you would find you were after all using a model.

*Duhemist:* I think I can do better than to appeal to a vaguely defined sense of "simplicity." We might realize strong falsifiability in the following way. Suppose we are given a number of accepted state-

ments correlating some of the $P$'s with some of the
$O$'s. If the consequences of the formal theory are
developed, it may be the case that the structure of
some of them appear formally similar to that of the
accepted statements, in the sense that a one-to-one
correspondence between symbols of the theory and
terms of the observation statements can be found.
It will then be possible to identify some of the $P$'s
with symbols of the theory. The theory can then be
said to explain the accepted correlations containing
these $P$-predicates, and it may also be capable of gen-
erating new and as yet unaccepted sentences containing the $P$'s, and therefore of making genuinely
new predictions. It was surely in some such way
that Maxwell's equations, developed for explanation
of electromagnetic phenomena, were seen to explain
also the transmission of light, because their solutions
were wave equations formally similar to equations
of the wave theory of light.

*Campbellian:* I can see some objections to this.
First, it is not clear what is meant by "the structure
of some of the consequences of the theory being formally similar to that of the accepted statements."
In a case such as that of Maxwell's equations it was
clear that there was such a similarity or isomorphism, and what the isomorphism consisted in. But
it is not easy to say in general how one would recognize a situation of isomorphism, for example, how
much formal manipulation of the theory would be
admitted before the identifications were found to be

possible? It might even be possible to show that the occurrence of isomorphism is trivial in the sense that *any* sufficiently rich theory could be made isomorphic with any given accepted statements, especially if these were simple and few in number.

You might, of course, be able to evade this objection by tightening up the formal criteria of isomorphism in some way, but even then it is not clear that success in finding an isomorphism would be sufficient in itself to confirm the wider applicability of the theory. Mere formal appearance of the wave equation in two different systems would not suffice to show a correlation in one theory, unless, as with Maxwell's equations, there were some interpretation which made it plausible to assume that one set of phenomena, the optical, was produced by the other, the electromagnetic—the interpretation in this case being that of wave propagation in the material ether. Whittaker gives the example of Mathieu's Equation, which appears in both the theory of elliptic membranes and the theory of equilibrium of an acrobat in a balancing act. It would not be suggested that any unification of theory is accomplished by noticing this fact.

Again, for your program to work significantly, there must already be a fairly well-developed system of relations in the observation language. The less developed this is, the more difficult it will be to ensure that an apparent isomorphism is not accidental or arbitrary. This means that the program will not be universally applicable and not applicable at all to observation predicates not already part of such a system in the observation language. It almost seems as though, for the formalist program to work at all, a previous stage of science making use of theories with models is necessary, in order that a sufficiently complex observation language shall have been built up. That this is the case would be admitted by those who regard classical physics as an observation language for which no further theoretical models are possible, even though classical physics itself consists of theories with models from the point of view of the observation language of common discourse.

The description you now give of the formalist program does not in any case provide necessary criteria for a theory, for, on the formalist view, it can never be more than a lucky accident that a satisfactory isomorphism is found. Whenever it is found, there is a spectacular unification of two or more previously disconnected fields, as in optics and electromagnetism, but such theoretical developments are exceptions which cannot be systematically sought for.

*Duhemist:* But of course we all know that the progress of science is not a mechanically systematic affair, but depends partly on hunches, intuitions, and guesswork, "lucky accidents" if you like, and I do not think my account involves a greater proportion of these than anybody else's. I am in fact prepared to accept that much of the progress of science does depend on these things and to say that the requirement

of falsifiability in sense *B* is too strong if it is taken
to mean that theories of this kind can be sought
for systematically. After all, spectacular predictions
in observational domains outside the original range
of a theory are in fact rare in science and cannot be
regarded as necessary logical conditions for a theory.
I suggest that whether a theory is required to be
falsifiable in this strong sense will depend on the initial complexity of the correlations in the observation
language. If this contains only the predicates of ordinary language, and prescientific correlations between
them, it is likely that weak falsifiability will not be
sufficient for a genuine theory. For if correlations
between only a few *O*'s are known, no theory of type
*A* will be able to predict any more, and a theory explaining the correlations between the *O*'s remains
imprisoned within the same limited observational
situations. If, however, the observation language is
already complex—if it is, for example, the language
of classical physics—then it is possible that the formal theory may go on for a long time providing interesting correlations between new observational
situations which are still described by the same predicates, between, for example, various kinds of particles described by the classical predicates "mass,"
"charge," and "spin." Parts of the theory of quantum mechanics may well be purely formal, and yet
falsifiable in this sense.

*Campbellian:* This is an interesting suggestion,
and it would need a far more detailed investigation

than we can undertake now. But I should like to
introduce some examples from quantum physics to
indicate that there may be more elements of model-
thinking in it than are recognized by your school of
thought. It is usually claimed that, at least on the
so-called Copenhagen view, quantum theory is an
example of an accepted and useful theory in which
models have been abandoned and which, therefore,
proves that models are not essential to the progress
of theories. And it is certainly true that the Copenhagen view can be regarded as a formalist view of
quantum theory in that it refrains from making any
interpretations of the formalism of the theory except
such as can be made directly in terms of classical
physics. It need not trouble us that what stands in
place of the observation language here is not ordinary descriptive language but the language of classical physics, which is from another point of view
highly theoretical, for we have already agreed that
what counts as an observation language is pragmat-
ically relative. But it does not follow that because
the adherents of the Copenhagen view refrain from
making interpretations when talking *about* quantum theory, they also avoid implicit interpretations
when actually using it in the process of research.
Many examples could be given from technical papers to show that they do not in fact avoid interpretations. Let me describe a comparatively simple one,
which is typical of the kind of argument that cannot be avoided when developments of the theory
are suggested.

In terms of classical physics, acting here as the observation language,  it is sometimes possible to describe certain phenomena as effects of charged particles, for example, electrons. It is never possible, however, to speak in classical terms of identifying an individual electron on different occasions or, in particular, of distinguishing the state of a system containing two electrons in given positions from that in which the electrons have changed places. According to the Copenhagen view, then, we must not make any interpretation implying anything about the identity of individual electrons. If, however, we do not adhere to this view, there are two possible interpretations of a situation in which an object cannot be re-identified, one exemplified by the $model_2$ of identical billiard balls, and the other by the $model_2$ of pounds, shillings, and pence in a bank balance. In the case of identical billiard balls, if we are not in a position to observe them continuously, we cannot in practice distinguish a situation in which two balls are in two given pockets from a situation at a later time in which they have changed places. But the two situations are in fact different, and if we were concerned with the number of arrangements of two balls in the two pockets, we should have to count them as two different arrangements. With pounds, shillings, and pence in a bank balance, however, it is not merely the case that we cannot in practice re-identify a given pound appearing in the credit column, but that there is no sense in speaking of the self-identity of this pound, and of asking where it reappears in another column or whether it is the pound paid over the counter yesterday. In this case the number of ways of arranging two unit pounds in different places in a column is just one, and there is no sense in speaking of another arrangement in which they have changed places. Units which behave in this way conform to the so-called Fermi-Dirac statistics, and not to the statistics of objects having self-identity.

If the Copenhagen view with regard to electrons were adhered to, we should be unable to say which of these two models of indistinguishability was appropriate, because we should not be in a position to use any models at all. But in fact we find the following argument very frequently used. We are unable to identify individual electrons, hence it is meaningless to speak of the self-identity of electrons, hence electrons are like pounds, shillings, and pence in a balance and not like indistinguishable billiard balls, and hence they conform to Fermi-Dirac statistics. The last step of this argument can be made to yield observable predictions, since there are various ways in which the behavior of entities satisfying Fermi-Dirac statistics is different in classically observable ways from those satisfying the statistics of ordinary objects. But the argument, in spite of its agnosticism about what cannot be observed, does in fact involve an interpretation and a choice between two different models, and without this choice the observable predictions cannot be derived. The crucial step from formalism to interpretation in the argument occurs when what the observer cannot do—namely, make certain distinction—is taken to be a property of the interpreted system, namely, that there is no such distinction. Such arguments are very commonly used in quantum theory to derive observable results and are sufficient to show that the theory is not as a whole a counter-example to the view that interpretations are essential for predictions.

Another example can be given to indicate the inadequacy of the Copenhagen view, which was developed to deal with the paradoxes of elementary quantum theory and has never been consistently adhered to in the later developments of quantum field theory. In the case of Dirac's prediction of the positron, not only was an interpretative theory successful, but also the same theory treated formally would have been refuted and discarded. The successful prediction arose as follows. The equations of motions of both classical and quantum charged particles admit of solutions representing particles with either positive or negative energy. In classical physics, however, the occurrence of negative energy solutions can be ignored, since in classical physics energy values change continuously, and if a particle is once taken to have positive energy it can never reach a negative-energy state. In quantum physics, however, energy changes take place discontinuously. Thus an electron may jump from one energy state to another, and negative states are as accessible as positive. Now, if the theory of these equations of motion is taken in a formal sense, the nonappearance of negative energy particles in any known experiment would count as a refutation of the theory. Dirac, however, made an interpretation of the theory which depended on the idea that each of the possible negative states is already filled by an electron which is not observable as long as it remains in this state, but which becomes observable if it is knocked out of the state, leaving a "hole" in the negative states which is also observable. By combining the two negatives provided by negative energy and the notion of "hole," the hole can be expected to behave like a particle of *positive* energy, and it will also have positive charge. This predicted particle, the positron, was in fact observed, and hence the interpreted theory both made a successful prediction and explained the previous nonappearance of negative energy particles which threatened to refute the theory regarded formally.

*Duhemist:* It may be true that there are still some preformalist arguments used in quantum theory, but you cannot maintain that in general quantum theory supports your case that models are essential. The fact that here the mathematical formalism may sometimes be usefully interpreted in terms of waves and sometimes in terms of particles, and that these models contradict each other although the formalism is self-consistent, shows that the models cannot be essential to the logic of the theory. The theory is here the formalism, not the partial interpretations, such as those in your examples, although these may be useful for special and limited problems.

*Campbellian:* I have to agree that the situation in quantum theory is peculiar from my point of view. Perhaps I can put it this way in the terminology I introduced earlier. The particle model (model$_2$) has some positive analogy with atomic phenomena and some negative analogy, and the same applies to the wave model$_2$. Much of the particle model's positive analogy is the wave model's negative analogy, and vice versa, and this is why the two models appear to be contradictory. If that were all there were to say, we could simply extract the two sets of positive analogies and drop all talk about particles and waves, but that is not all there is to say, because in both cases there are still features about which we do not know whether they are positive or negative analogies. And it is in arguing in terms of these features that the particle and wave models are still essential, supplemented by the hunches physicists have acquired about when to argue in terms of one and when the other. And, as you have suggested earlier, developments in quantum theory which appear to be novel (in the sense of falsifiability *B*) may actually be results of novel deductions within parts of the theory already interpreted, and hence be only what I have called extensions of type *A*. These are surely going to yield diminishing returns, and any quantum theorist who adopts my point of view on models will presumably be dissatisfied with the state of the theory until a new model is found incorporating the positive analogies of both particles and waves, but not involving their contradictions. But I don't suppose either of us wishes to rest his arguments on current disputes in quantum theory or on speculations about its future.

*Duhemist:* It sometimes seems that our whole dispute reduces to a difference of opinion about what kind of theory will predominate in the future, and this is rather unprofitable to speculate upon. I think, however, that you have been forced to admit that important extensions of theory *may* take place without the use of models, and so you have effectively admitted that models are not logically essential. You could only continue to maintain that they are by showing that all my examples of formal methods are either unacceptable or not purely formal, and this you have not done. For my part, I can see that it may be possible and useful to analyze in more detail what is involved in using models when they are used and to enquire whether there is any justification for expecting more systematic theory-construction with their aid than without. This would be an extension of inductive logic in application to the hypothetico-deductive structure of theories. I must confess that in view of the inconclusive results of inductive logic in the simpler case of empirical generalizations, I am not very optimistic about the success of such an investigation.

*Campbellian:* I think two sorts of problems have to be distinguished here. There is the general problem of the justification of induction, of which the problem of justifying the inference to hypotheses by means of models would be a special case, and I agree that the history of inductive logic does not make the prospects for this very bright. But there are subsidiary problems to this, namely, to find the conditions for the assertion of an analogy, to elucidate the nature of arguments using models and analogies, and to compare these arguments with those usually called inductive in a more general sense. These problems arise on your view of the nature of theories as well as on mine, because even if models are merely dispensable aids to discovery it is still profitable to ask how they work, and if this is to be called a "psychological" investigation, it may be none the worse for that. Certainly the use of models is not psychological in the sense of being wholly an individual and subjective matter, since communication and argument often go on between scientists in terms of models, and if this shows no more than a uniformity in the scientific temperament, it is still worth investigating.

It does not, of course, follow that such an investigation will provide anything like an infallible method for the construction of theories, any more than it is the intention of accounts of methods of induction to provide infallible induction machines. All that is being attempted is an analysis of what assumptions are made when analogies are used in science, and how it is that certain hypotheses rather than others suggest themselves "by analogy." Whether the hypotheses thus suggested turn out to be *true* is, as always, a matter for empirical investigation. The logic of analogy, like the logic of induction, may be descriptive without being justificatory.

# Material Analogy

Two questions raised in our dialogue now require more detached investigation:

1. What is an analogy?
2. When is an argument from analogy valid?

It is characteristic of modern, as opposed to classical and medieval logic, that the answer to the first question is taken to be either obvious or unanalyzable, while the second is taken to be a question involving induction, and therefore highly problematic. In classical and medieval logic, on the other hand, there is a certain amount of analysis of types of analogy, but practically no attempt at justification of the validity of analogical arguments, although such arguments are frequently used. And since neither the classical types of analogy nor the sketchily defined analogies of modern logic bear much resemblance to analogy as used in reasoning from scientific models,[1] we need to examine the relation of this problem to the traditional discussions. I shall, then, put forward a definition of the analogy *relation* in this chapter, and go on to consider the justification of analogical *argument* in the next.

It is as well to begin by considering very briefly

1. In this chapter, the sense of "model" will always be model$_2$ of the first chapter unless otherwise stated.

examples of various types of analogy from the literature in order to bring out the main issues.

*Example A.* An analogy may be said to exist between two objects in virtue of their common properties. Take, for example, the earth and the moon.
Both are large, solid, opaque, spherical bodies, re-
ceiving heat and light from the sun, revolving on
their axes, and gravitating toward other bodies.
These properties may be said to constitute their
positive analogy. On the other hand, the moon is
smaller than the earth, more volcanic, and has no
atmosphere and no water. In these respects there is
negative analogy between them. Thus the question
of what the analogy is in this case is fully answered
by pointing to the positive and negative analogies,
and the discussion passes immediately to the second
question. Under what circumstances can we argue
from, for example, the presence of human beings on
the earth to their presence on the moon? The validity of such an argument will depend, first, on the
extent of the positive analogy compared with the
negative (for example, it is stronger for Venus than
for the moon, since Venus is more similar to the
earth) and, second, on the relation between the new
property and the properties already known to be
parts of the positive or negative analogy, respectively. If we have reason to think that the properties in the positive analogy are causally related, in a
favorable sense, to the presence of humans on the
earth, the argument will be strong. If, on the other

hand, the properties of the moon which are parts of
the negative analogy tend causally to *prevent* the
presence of humans on the moon the argument will
be weak or invalid.

I shall return to this type of argument later, but
meanwhile two features of the analogy should be
noted. First, there is a one-to-one relation of identity
or difference between a property of one of the analogues and a corresponding property of the other
and, second, the relation between properties of the
same analogue is that of being properties of the same
object, together with causal relations between these
properties. Schematically:

|  | EARTH | MOON |
|---|---|---|
| causal relations | ↑ spherical . . . . . spherical | |
| | atmosphere . . . . no atmosphere | |
| | ↓ humans . . . . . . . ? | |

←――――――→
relations of identity
or difference

We shall find that a common feature of all the
analogies we discuss will be the appearance of two
sorts of dyadic relation, and I shall call these *horizontal* and *vertical relations,* respectively. Thus, horizontal relations will be concerned with identity and
difference, as in this case, or in general with *similarity,* and vertical relations will, in most cases, be
*causal.*

*Example B.* Consider next the scientific analogy already referred to in the last chapter, between the properties of light and of sound. Here again we have two lists of properties, with some members of one list corresponding to some members of the other:

|  | PROPERTIES OF SOUND | PROPERTIES OF LIGHT |
|---|---|---|
| ↑ | echoes | reflection |
| causal relations | loudness | brightness |
| | pitch | color |
| | detected by ear | detected by eye |
| ↓ | propagated in air | propagated in "ether" |

⋮  ←——————→  ⋮

similarity relations

In this example, unlike *A,* there is no clear division of the two lists into identities and differences, since the pairs of corresponding terms are never identical but only *similar.* There are, of course, some terms on both sides that have no corresponding term on the other, but I shall regard these as special cases of "similars," where the similarity relation is defined so as to include identities and differences. The vertical relations between members of the same list are, as in example *A,* causal relations.

It has been suggested in the previous chapter that this analogy, like *A,* can be used in arguments from similarities in some respects to similarity in respect of a property known to belong to one analogue but not yet known to belong to the other. For example, known similarities in properties of reflection, refraction, and intensity may lead to a prediction regarding color from properties involving pitch or from the properties of air to those of "ether." Here, however, the situation is more complicated than in example *A,* in that it may not be initially obvious *which* property of light corresponds with which property of sound (why do we make color correspond with pitch?), or it may be that a particular property of sound has *no* correlate among the properties of light, in which case one may be invented ("ether" is initially not *observed* as the obvious correlate of air, it is rather *postulated* to fill the place of a missing correlate among the properties of light). Thus in this example, unlike the first, the question of defining the analogy relation and hence identifying its terms must come before the question of justification of the analogical argument.

*Example C.* Consider next an analogy in a classification system, of a kind first stated explicitly by Aristotle:

| *Genera* | BIRD | FISH |
|---|---|---|
|  | wing | fin |
|  | lungs | gills |
|  | feathers | scales |
|  | ⋮ | ⋮ |

Here the horizontal relation may be one or more or several similarities of structure or of function, and each list may contain some items which have no, or no obvious, correspondent in the other list; for example, without anatomical investigation it is not clear that birds' legs correspond to anything in the structure of fish. The vertical relations may be conceived as no more than that of whole to its parts, or they may be regarded as causal relations depending on some theory or interrelation of parts determined by evolutionary origin or adaptation to environment. In this latter case, the analogy may be used predictively as in the previous example—to argue, for instance, from the known structure of a bird's skeleton to missing parts of a fish skeleton. But again the nature of the analogy relation itself requires elucidation before considering the validity of the argument.

*Example D.* Finally, an example of a kind used and misused in political rhetoric brings out by contrast some important characteristics of the three previous examples:

$$\frac{\text{father}}{\text{children}} :: \frac{\text{state}}{\text{citizens}}$$

An analogy of this kind is apparently an assertion that the relation between father and child is the same in many respects as that between state and citizens, for example, in that the father is responsible for the maintenance, welfare, and defense of the child; and it is further implied that it follows from this that other relations should also be the same, for example that the citizen owes respect and obedience to the state. There are several differences between this example and the previous ones. First of all, its purpose is persuasive rather than predictive. It is not arguing from three known terms to one unknown, as is the case in the first three examples; it is rather pointing out the consequences, of a moral or normative character, which follow from the relations of four terms already known. Second, the vertical relation is not specifically causal. There are in fact several vertical relations, provider-for, protector-of, and so on; and the argument implicitly passes from asserting some such relations which are already recognized to persuading the hearer that other relations (obedient-to, etc.) follow from these. Third, there does not seem to be any horizontal relation of similarity between the terms, except in virtue of the fact that the two pairs are related by the same vertical relation. That is to say, there is no horizontal relation *independent* of the vertical relations, and here this example differs from all the other three types, where the horizontal relations of similarity were independent of the vertical and could be recognized before the vertical relations were known. It seems to be exclusively analogies of this kind that Richard Robinson is thinking of when he asserts that analogy in any sense other than mathematical proportionality "is merely the fact that some relations have more than one example,"[2] that is that "$a$ is to $b$ as $c$ is to

2. *Rev. Metaphysics,* V, 1952, 466.

$d''$ is merely equivalent to asserting the existence of a relation $R$ such that $aRb$ and $cRd$. But Robinson overlooks analogies of the other kinds we have mentioned, where there are similarity relations $aSc$ and $bS'd$ independent of the vertical relations.

## ANALOGY AND MATHEMATICAL PROPORTION

At this point we can usually draw a distinction between the types of analogy we are concerned with and the relation of mathematical proportionality. The two kinds of relation have often been thought to be closely connected, as is indicated by the fact that the Greek word for "proportion" is *analogia*. And the relations do indeed have some formal resemblances, which have been presupposed in the notation for the four-term relation already adopted in the previous chapter.

Let us represent the relation "*a* is to *b* as *c* is to *d*" by $\dfrac{a}{b} :: \dfrac{c}{d}$, where $a$ and $b$ are any two terms taken from a list representing one analogue in examples *A, B,* or *C,* including the heading, and $c$ and $d$ are the corresponding terms taken from the other list. For example, "pitch is to sound as color is to light," "wing is to bird as fin is to fish," or "wing is to feather as fin is to scales":

$$\frac{\text{pitch}}{\text{sound}} :: \frac{\text{color}}{\text{light}}, \quad \frac{\text{wing}}{\text{bird}} :: \frac{\text{fin}}{\text{fish}}, \quad \frac{\text{wing}}{\text{feathers}} :: \frac{\text{fin}}{\text{scales}}.$$

This generalized analogy relation has the following formal characteristics in common with numerical proportionality:

1. We wish to say that the analogy relation is *reflexive,* that is to say $\frac{a}{b} :: \frac{a}{b}$, although this is a trivial case of the general relation.

2. We wish to say that the analogy relation is *symmetrical,* for if $\frac{a}{b} :: \frac{c}{d}$, then $\frac{c}{d} :: \frac{a}{b}$.

3. We wish to say that the analogy relation can be *inverted,* for if $\frac{a}{b} :: \frac{c}{d}$, then $\frac{b}{a} :: \frac{d}{c}$.

4. We can compare the additive property of numerical proportion with the results of taking the *logical sum* of terms of an analogy. Just as we have in numerical proportion that if $\frac{a}{b} = \frac{c}{d}$ then $\frac{a+b}{b} = \frac{c+d}{d}$, so it is convenient to say, for example, that

$$\frac{\text{properties of sound}}{\text{pitch}} :: \frac{\text{properties of light}}{\text{color}}$$

where "properties of sound" and "properties of light" are taken to be just logical sums of terms in their respective lists.

5. Locating a corresponding term in an analogy has some resemblance to finding the fourth term of a proportionality, given the other three terms. Suppose we are given three terms of an analogy, say *a, b, c,*

where $a$ and $b$ specify a vertical relation, say $aRb$, and $c$ is the term corresponding to $a$ in another analogue. Location of a fourth term can then occur in two different ways. If we know the relations between terms of this other analogue, we may locate $d$ such that $cRd$ from the given $c$ and $R$. This will be the case in example $B$ when we already know the wave-theory relations between pitch and other properties of sound, and between color and other properties of light. The analogy will then tell us that color corresponds to pitch. Or we may not know the causal relations in the second set of terms, and then we have to look for a $d$ related to $b$ by similarity. This will be the case in the pretheoretic use of example $B$, where we look for that property of light which has some similarity with pitch (for example, has similar effects on our sense organs). Or again, in example $C$, wing and fin are similar in structure and function, therefore the required term corresponding to lungs will be similar in one or both of these respects to lungs.

Here, however, the resemblance between proportion and analogy ends. Even the resemblance just discussed under (5) is not complete, for it may not be the case that the analogy relation gives a *unique* fourth term. For example, we may think that birds' legs or birds' tails are equally good analogues for fishes' tails, so that both would provide a fourth term in "fish is to fishtail as bird is to . . . ," each corresponding to similarities in different respects.

Another difference between proportion and analogy arises from the fact that the horizontal and vertical relations are relations of the same kind in proportion, but not in analogy. This means, among other things, that the terms of an analogy cannot be alternated without producing a relation of a different kind, for if $\frac{a}{b} :: \frac{c}{d}$ is replaced by $\frac{a}{c} :: \frac{b}{d}$ , the relation no longer conforms to the convention that horizontal relations are relations of similarity, and vertical relations are causal. Finally, in analogy, unlike proportion, there is not, in general, transitivity between three pairs of terms, for if $\frac{a}{b} :: \frac{c}{d}$ and $\frac{c}{d} :: \frac{e}{f}$ , there may be no analogy relation at all, or anyway not such a close one, between $\frac{a}{b}$ and $\frac{e}{f}$. This is due to the dependence of analogy on similarity, for it is not in general the case that two things which are each similar to a third thing are similar to each other. They may be similar to the third thing in different respects, or, if in the same respect, their respective similarities to the third thing may be much greater than their similarity to each other.

## THE SIMILARITY RELATION

The examples $A$ to $D$ do not by any means exhaust all possible types of analogy and analogical argument, but they are sufficient to indicate the boundaries that can be drawn round the present enquiry into analogical reasoning from scientific models. We have seen that analogy is used in two senses in physical theories—there is the one-to-one correspondence between different interpretations of the same formal theory, which we may call *formal analogy,* and there are pretheoretic analogies between observables such as

$$\frac{\text{properties of sound}}{\text{pitch}} :: \frac{\text{properties of light}}{\text{color}}$$

which enable predictions to be made from a model. Let us call this second sense *material analogy.*

It is clearly the notion of material analogy which causes most of the difficulties, and it is this type of analogy which is required if prediction from models is to be possible in the strong sense of the last chapter. One of the questions left unanswered there was whether the above example about sound and light can be counted as an analogy at all, except in the formal posttheoretic sense. It is already clear that if there is a sense of analogy other than the formal here, this must be in virtue of some kind of similarity between the horizontal terms. Examples $A$ to $D$ include two extreme cases of the similarity relation, both of which are instructive. Example $D$ is a case of no horizontal similarity independent of the vertical relation, and in this respect it is paralleled exactly by *formal* analogy in science, for there two terms related by analogy need have no similarity other than that of both being interpretations of the same term in a formal theory, that is, of being corresponding *relata* in the *vertical* causal network of relations constituting the theory. An example of such an analogy was given in our first chapter—the formal analogy between elliptic membranes and the acrobat's equilibrium, both of which are described by Mathieu's Equation. This analogy is useless for prediction precisely because there is no similarity between corresponding terms. At the other extreme in respect of similarity is example *A*. Here there is not merely *similarity* between the properties related horizontally in the positive analogy, for they are the *same* property. This contrasts with the pairs of terms in the other examples—"wing" and "fin," and "pitch" and "color"—in which members of a pair are not only not identical, but it is often not clear in what their similarity consists or what term of a given analogue should be paired with what in virtue of their similarity. The fact that most modern logical accounts of analogy have been carried out only with examples like *A* or *D* in mind, explains why the *nature* of the analogical relation has not been thought to be problematic.

It should be noticed that if material analogies between models and explicanda are to do the predictive job required of them, they must be *observable* similarities between corresponding terms and must not depend on a theory of the explicandum. Thus, the colliding-elastic-ball model for gases suggests itself in the first place because of observable similarities between, for example, the behavior of bouncing balls and bouncing balloons, and between the effects of pressure on a surface due to a hail of particles and those due to an expanding gas. The pretheoretic similarities between pitch and color are rather less obvious, but a good deal of support can be gathered from the history of theories of sound and light for the assertion that such similarities were recognized before any theory having the same formal characteristics for both sound and light was known. Aristotle, for instance, based his conjecture of the analogy between pitch and color on the observed facts that certain combinations of sounds and certain mixtures of colors are pleasant to the senses and others unpleasant, and that excess of brightness or darkness, or of sharp or flat, destroys the senses.

These examples suggest that when similarities are recognized they are described in some such way as, "Both analogues have property $B$, but whereas the first has property $A$, the second has instead property $C$."[3] It may be that when the nature of the similarity is pressed, it will be admitted that the analogues do not both have the *identical* property $B$, but two *similar* properties, say $B$ and $B'$, in which

3. "Having a property $A$" is here regarded as an *intensional* characteristic of an analogue. No attempt is made to give a purely extensional analysis either of properties or of relations of identity and difference between them. But once objects have been sorted into classes by recognition of their intensional properties, these classes can, as far as the *logical* discussion is concerned, be regarded as defining the properties, and extensional interpretation applied throughout.

case the analysis of the similarity of $B$ and $B'$ repeats the same pattern. But if we suppose that at some point this analysis stops, with the open or tacit assumption that further consideration of difference between otherwise identical properties can be ignored, we have an analysis of similarity into relations of identity and difference. And only if this is the case can we assimilate arguments from similarities between model and explicandum to what traditional logic has called "argument from analogy," of which a classic example is $A$, and which depends only on identities and differences.

In terms of such an analysis the general schema for the four examples we have considered becomes:

| ANALOGUE $x$ | ANALOGUE $y$ |
|---|---|
| $A_1(x)B_1(x)$ | $B_1(y)C_1(y)$ |
| $A_2(x)B_2(x)$ | $B_2(y)C_2(y)$ |
| $\vdots \quad \vdots$ | $\vdots \quad \vdots$ |

Let us call the predicates $A_1$, $A_2$, $B_1$ etc., *characters*. Example $A$ of analogy now becomes the special case in which there are no characters such as the $A$'s and $C$'s, which occur in one list and not in the other, and example $D$ is the special case in which there are no characters such as the $B$'s which occur in both lists.

But why place the characters in groups rather than list them singly as identities or differences between the two analogues as in example $A$? The reason for this formulation is not fundamental but is connected with the way in which the characters present themselves at a given stage of empirical enquiry. Let us consider the earth-moon example, in which the characters are listed as simple identities or differences.

If it is said (as by Mill) that the validity of the analogical argument depends on the known causal relations between the properties of both analogues, two situations may arise. Either (as in the case of the conditions for human life) the causal relations are known *independently* of either of the analogues, in which case the argument for or against human life on the moon is an ordinary causal argument from universal laws of nature applied in a particular instance, the moon, and the earth is irrelevant to the argument; or else the only causal relations known are those implied by the co-occurrence of certain properties on the earth, in which case the argument looks like an enumerative induction which is very weak because based on only one instance. But neither of these alternatives is a satisfactory analysis of analogical argument; the first because it does away with the argument derived from the similarity of the analogues altogether; the other because it represents analogical argument merely as a weak induction from a single instance.

But analogical argument is not just inductive generalization, and any account which reduces it to this is misleading. Expressing the matter more formally, the analogical argument consists in the following: given two analogues $x$ and $y$ which resemble each other in a number of characters $B_1 \ldots B_m$, and are dissimilar in that $x$ also has $A_1 \ldots A_n$ and $y$ has not, and $y$ has also $C_1 \ldots C_l$ and $x$ has not, we want to know whether another character $D$ of $x$ is likely to belong also to $y$. This will be called the *logical problem* of analogy. (For brevity we refer to the characters in intensional notation and leave their arguments $x$ and $y$ to be understood. The translation to extensional notation is obvious throughout.)

If the casual relations of $A_1 \ldots A_n$ with $D$, and $B_1 \ldots B_m$ with $D$ are known independently of each other, and, in particular, independently of $x$, then the inference to possession of $D$ by $y$ is purely causal and need make no reference to $x$. This is the situation in the earth-moon example, since in that case enough is known of the causal relation of, for example, atmosphere to life, to make this relation a universal law, independent of the particular co-occurrence of atmosphere and human life on the earth. Hence the inference that human life cannot occur on the moon follows simply from the absence on the moon of one of its causally necessary conditions. But this is not always the situation, and in particular is not the situation in analogical reasoning from scientific models. In a system $x$ which is to be used as a model for a theory about an explicandum $y$, we do not generally know the causal relations of the $A$'s with $D$ and the $B$'s with $D$ *separately*, we only know that $D$ is related to the $A$'s and $B$'s as they occur together in the model. For example, if an elastic ball is taken as a model for sound, we know that when a ball is thrown against a wall it rebounds, but we cannot empirically separate the characteristics which are in common between the throwing of a ball and the uttering of a sound, and those which are different, in order to infer a general causal relation applicable also to sound: "throwing is correlated with rebound," in such a way that this is independent of the occurrence of the other characters of the ball. It is this practical impossibility of empirically separating some of the characters from others that has dictated the form in which characters have been listed for each analogue in the table just given.

Another point should be made here about the relations of induction and analogical argument. There is a well-known chicken-and-egg paradox which can be expressed as follows: argument from analogy depends on induction from known laws connecting the properties of each analogue; hence all such argument is inductive. On the other hand, inductive argument depends on recognizing similarities between instances, none of which is in practice exactly the same as the others; hence all such argument is analogical. The regress may be stopped, however, if we agree to admit characters between which we recognize identities or differences which we take to be not further analyzable. Then an inductive argument will be one from a large number of instances of which a typical one may be represented by $B_1 \ldots B_m C_{r1} \ldots C_{rl}$, where $B_1 \ldots B_m$ are identical for all instances, and $C_{r1} \ldots C_{rl}$ is a set of characters which differentiates the $r$th instance from the others. When $B_1 \ldots B_m$ have been found to occur together in a large number of instances, each containing different sets of $C$'s, we conclude that we can ignore the $C$'s in forming inductive arguments about the $B$'s. In an analogical argument, however, we have *one* set of $B$'s and *one* set of $C$'s presented together, and we do not know, and are not in a position to find out, whether the relations between the $B$'s remain the same in the absence of the $C$'s. Thus inductive argument is more fundamental than analogical. But this does not mean that inductive argument requires instances to repeat themselves exactly, which never happens; it merely requires us to be able to discriminate among characters which are presented together those which are relevant to the argument (because they have retained constant mutual relations in many otherwise different instances), and those which are not (because they have varied from instance to instance).

This point also helps to answer another objection. It may be said that it is impossible to discriminate characters which are always presented together, as is assumed to be the case in analogical argument. But if this were so, it would never be possible to recognize more than one instance of the same inductive generalization, for we should never recognize $B_1 \ldots B_m$ in association with $C_{11} \ldots C_{1l}$ as the same

$B_1 \ldots B_m$ that we next find in association with $C_{21} \ldots C_{2k}$. It is essential for both inductive and analogical arguments that the characters are separately *recognizable* although they may never be separately presented. The difference between the two types of argument is due to the amount of information available, and analogical argument is necessary only in situations where it has not been possible to observe or to produce experimentally a large number of instances in which sets of characters are differently associated. In other words, it is necessary in situations where Bacon's or Mill's methods of agreement and difference cannot be applied. Thus, in a sense analogical argument is "weaker" than inductive, but on the other hand it has the advantage of being applicable where straightforward generalization is not.

Of course the description of similarities and differences between two analogues is a notoriously inaccurate, incomplete, and inconclusive procedure. Although we often feel some confidence in asserting the existence of a similarity and that some things are more similar to each other than to other things, we cannot usually locate discrete characteristics in one object which are positively and finally identifiable with or differentiable from those in another object. But the inconclusive nature of the procedure is not fatal here, because we are not looking for incorrigible inductive methods, but only for methods of selecting *hypotheses*. Analogical argument is inconclusive, both for the usual inductive reasons and also because it may rest on incomplete location of similarities; nevertheless, as will be argued in the next chapter, it does provide a method of hypothesis-selection which is justifiable on at least some of the recognized criteria for such selection. Further, we shall see that even if it were possible accurately to *weight* the similarities between an explicandum and different models which are compared with it, this would not strengthen the analogical argument according to any of its acceptable justifications, and so it is pointless even to seek to define *degrees* of similarity among the sets of characters.

## THE CAUSAL RELATION

An argument from analogy requires a certain kind of similarity relation between the horizontal terms of the analogy, and also a certain kind of vertical relation. The examples $C$ and $D$ indicate the existence of analogies where the dyadic vertical relation or relations may be of many different kinds: whole-to-part, organism-to-organ, protector-of, obedient-to, and so on; most of which are not obviously causal in the sense in which the relation of "atmosphere" to "humans" or "wave-motion" to "reflection" is causal. But what, more precisely, is this sense? It is at least a tendency to co-occurrence. In the case of the relation "atmosphere" to "humans," the first term is, or is claimed to be, a necessary condition of the second; that is to say, the occurrence of one of the terms is a causal condition of the occurrence of the other.

The same can be said of the relations between the properties of a model such as elastic balls or sound waves. Certain properties are necessary or sufficient conditions for other properties, and the network of causal relations thus established will make the occurrence of one property at least tend, subject to the presence of other properties, to promote or inhibit the occurrence of another. Arguments from models involve those analogies which can be used to predict the *occurrence* of certain properties or events, and hence the relevant relations are causal, at least in the sense of implying a tendency to co-occur. Dyadic relations in which the empirical occurrence of one of the relata implies nothing about the occurrence of the other will not justify analogical inference. For example, it may be said that "man is to woman as boy is to girl," but the occurrence of a man, a woman, and a boy, gives in itself no grounds for expecting the occurrence of a girl. And, as we shall see, it can be argued that the mere placing of terms in a classification system, as in example *C*, gives a sense to the relation of analogy, but gives in itself no grounds for inferring from the existence of entities represented by three of the terms to the existence of an entity represented by the fourth.

Within the requirement of tendency to co-occurrence, the causal relation may be analyzed in a number of ways. It may be represented in terms of a Humean relative frequency of co-occurrence in which closeness of causal connection between $A$ and $B$ corresponds to a high proportion of occurrences of $A$ and $B$ together as compared with their occurrences apart. (Some restrictions will be placed on this interpretation later.) Or the analysis of cause may be carried out in terms of a hypothetico-deductive theory, in which the causal relation between $A$ and $B$ follows as a law from some higher-level hypothesis. Or a cause $A$ may be interpreted modally, as in some sense *necessary* for $B$, or even ontologically, as in some sense *productive* of $B$. It is not my purpose here to go into the difficulties involved in these interpretations of cause, because in analyzing the nature of analogical argument in general, it is only necessary to point out that the argument, if valid, carries over the *same* sense of causal relation from model to explicandum, in virtue of the relations between the characters which model and explicandum share.

In whatever way the causal relation is interpreted, it is necessary to stress again that in the logical problem of analogy, the characters we are concerned with are not hidden causes or theoretical entities but *observables*. This is because, as well as being causally related within one analogue, they must, as we have seen, also be the characters in virtue of which similarities are recognized between superficially distinct causal systems. An analogical argument from models may lead to the discovery of hidden causes or to the postulation of theoretical entities, but the similarities from which it starts must be observable. Again, it should not be supposed that the characters are necessarily some kind of atomic constituents, combining to form the system by connection of parts, although they may sometimes be this. But in general we are not in a position observably to identify the atomic constituents of the systems we investigate, and, in any case, the characters in many of the examples we have discussed are not parts or constituents, and the systems are not constructed by connecting them. Thus sound is not *composed of* reflection, loudness, pitch, etc. But the whole-part relationship is not in general implied by the representation of a system by means of characters. All that is implied in representing a system as, for example $ABD$, is that the characters $A$, $B$, $D$ are causally related according to some acceptable interpretation of causality, which may be a relation of whole-part, as in the case of an organism and its organs, or may be co-occurrence and concomitant variation described by a set of empirical laws, as in such cases as elastic balls, gases, sound, and light.

The requirement of "an acceptable interpretation of causality" raises another point. This acceptability is not only a question of the philosophical analysis of causality, but also of the correctness of the assertion of a causal relation of given type between the actual terms of the analogy. Analogical arguments may be attacked not only on the grounds that they depend on superficial similarities, but also on the grounds that the causal relations assumed are inappropriate to the subject matter. These two forms of objection must be carefully distinguished. The second form of attack is based on disagreement about whether the connections asserted in the model do after all deserve to be called causal, or perhaps whether, though they may be appropriately causal for the model, they are proper to the subject matter of the explicandum. This is not specifically a disagreement about analogical argument, but about what kinds of theories or laws are to be admitted into different branches of science.

One form of this problem is illustrated by example *C*. In nineteenth-century biology definitions were elaborated of *homologies* and *analogies* in different species and groups of species. Roughly, organs in different species are *homologous* when they are structurally the same organ, that is, correspond in position and connections relative to the whole organism and are made up of corresponding parts, whatever difference there may be between their functions. In this sense the human hand and the bat's wing are homologous. Parts or organs are said to be *analogous* when they have the same function, whether or not they are also homologous; for example, the bat's wing and the bird's wing are analogous but are not structurally the same, and therefore are not homologous. Both "homology" and "analogy" can be said to be analogies in the sense of our material analogies, the difference being that in "homology" the horizontal relations are primarily similarities of structure, and in "analogy" they are similarities of function. In these biological analogies what constitutes the horizontal relation of similarity is in general clear enough; what is more problematic is the nature of the vertical relations.

Here it is necessary to be clear about the ways in which homologies and analogies have actually been used in biology. Generally speaking, the characteristics of the two species to be compared are known, and the similarities are used as indications of a "natural" classification, in which species showing greater similarity are grouped together. If the aim is merely to arrive at a convenient classification, little more needs to be said. The debates arise when this aim is extended in one of two directions. First, it may be desired to define more closely what is meant by a "natural" classification and to justify the classification arrived at in terms of this; or, second, it may be desired to predict from knowledge of one species, together with partial knowledge of another species homologous or analogous to it, the detailed characteristics of the latter. What is then required is some acceptable causal relation as a basis of the classification or as a causal justification of the prediction.

When homologies were first described in detail by Goethe, Cuvier, Saint-Hilaire and their successors, it was commonly suggested that community of type among organisms is based on an "ideal type," an archetype, or natural plan. If this is taken in an entirely Platonic sense, as not asserting the actual existence of an empirical thing, it can be criticized as being merely an ad hoc description of observed similarities, and therefore as not providing any proper theoretical basis of classification or prediction. On this view, no argument from analogy to the characteristics of a partially unknown species could be justified.

But the ideal type might be allowed to count as an acceptable causal theory if it could be shown to satisfy some of the usual criteria for a satisfactory scientific theory. The ideal type is at least a representation of frequent co-occurrences of some factors in organisms which are otherwise different. This in itself is not likely to be thought strong enough to provide a causal relation, but it may suggest that a stronger causal relation is present and can be looked for. Thus Cuvier, discussing the observed correlations between ruminants, cloven hooves and frontal horns, has no functional theory to explain this, and is no believer in evolution, and yet he takes frequency of co-occurrence to be sufficient indication of the existence of some *causal* relation stronger than co-occurrence. "Nevertheless, since these relations are constant, they must necessarily have a sufficient cause; but as we are ignorant of this cause, observation must supplement theory; observation establishes empirical laws which become almost as certain as the rational laws, when they are based upon a sufficient number of observations."[4]

The use of analogical argument presupposes a stronger causal relation than mere co-occurrence, as we shall see in the next chapter, but it does not presuppose that the actual causal relation is known. The ideal type might be regarded simply as a formal scheme derived from some of the observed species and then found to be applicable to others. This would already rescue it from the charge of being ad hoc. But further grounds for using homologies and analogies predictively would be provided if more general forms of theoretical explanation were given in the case of some of the species, just as the argument from a sound model to light is strengthened when the important characters in the model are picked out by a wave explanation of sound. Cuvier made use of a "principle of correlation," according to which functional analogies are derived from those correlations of parts of organisms which are necessary if the organisms are to be viable in the same type of environment and which are therefore repeated in different species. Or evolutionary theories may regard homologies as evidence of common descent, in which case the ideal type is justified by corresponding to the characteristics of an empirically existing ancestor, for which there may be independent evidence.

The scientific validity of an analogical argument

4. *Recherches sur les ossemens fossiles*, 1812, i, p. 63; quoted in E. S. Russell, *Form and Function* (London; 1916), p. 37.

from structural homologies or functional analogies will therefore depend partly on whether the connections asserted between the characters in common are regarded as scientifically acceptable causal connections. The logical argument rests on the presumption that if $AB$ is connected with $D$ in the model, then there is some possibility that $B$ is connected with $D$, and that this connection will tend to make $D$ occur with $BC$ in the explicandum. But if the relation between $AB$ and $D$ in the model is not itself regarded as more than an accidental co-occurrence, then no transfer of causality by an analogical argument will be admitted, because there is no causality to transfer.

A different form of the causal objection may arise when the analogy contains pairs of terms from different categories or different "ontological levels." It may then be argued that although the causal connections between characters in the model are acceptable, they cannot be carried over to the explicandum because the explicandum cannot be subject to the same kind of causality. An example can be suggested from cosmology, where it is often argued that properties which are properly ascribed to parts of the universe cannot be used as analogues for properties of the universe as a whole. This would make it impossible to argue from models involving, for example, conservation laws, finite time-span, increasing entropy, etc. to theories of the universe as a whole, even if there is some other observed, positive analogy between the universe as a whole and models taken from its parts. Again, this is not a dispute about the logical validity of analogical argument as such, but about the acceptability of certain causal relations.

The same kind of problem arises in a more extreme form in the attempts to draw analogies between human and divine, created and creator, which were the motive for a large part of medieval discussion of analogy. The suggested relation

$$\frac{\text{sculptor}}{\text{statue}} :: \frac{\text{God}}{\text{world}}$$

for example, has been objected to on the grounds (among others) that the causal relation asserted between God and the world *cannot,* in principle, be identical with that between sculptor and statue. And if this is the case, then it follows that this is not an analogy relation in the sense defined here, because it means that whatever similarity relations may be asserted between the terms in horizontal pairs, they do not carry causal relations from one analogue to the other.

### CONDITIONS FOR A MATERIAL ANALOGY

The conditions for a material analogy between scientific model$_2$ and explicandum may now be summarized as follows.

1. The horizontal dyadic relations between terms are relations of similarity, where similarity can, at least for purposes of analysis, be reduced to identities

and differences between sets of characters making up the terms.

2. The vertical relations in the model are causal relations in some acceptable scientific sense, where there are no compelling a priori reasons for denying that causal relations *of the same kind* may hold between terms of the explicandum.

These conditions have been suggested by analysis of examples of the use of models which make theories strongly predictive in the sense defined in the first chapter. The question now arises, are these conditions *necessary* and *sufficient* for this predictive use of models? Three kinds of counter-examples suggest themselves, the first to the assertion that the conditions are necessary, and the others to the assertion that they are sufficient.

*Conceptual Models*

Suppose we are given a model satisfying condition (1) and having a neutral analogy with the explicandum which can be exploited to make predictions, but which is *wholly imaginary*—that is, which is not realized in any existing or, as far as we know, any possible physical system. Such a conceptual model might be merely a modification of existing systems, whose behavior could be deduced from an existing causal theory, as, for instance, in the case of idealizations. In this case the model does satisfy condition (2) as well as condition (1), in virtue of the causal relations in the deductive theory, and so it does not constitute a counter-example to the necessity of both conditions. But suppose the model is not derived in any way from a causal theory and that the relations asserted to hold between its terms are wholly imaginary. Might it not still function as a model₂ in suggesting new predictions in the domain of the explicandum? An example would be the imaginary ideal types described in the last section, if we suppose that *no* evolutionary or other causal theory is suggested to justify them. Or suppose we design on paper, or actually build in the solid, a pattern of elements interpreted as constituents of the atomic nucleus and invent dynamic interrelations between them without appealing to any known causal laws. In some such way, at an early stage of atomic theory, John Dalton says he set himself "to combine my atoms upon paper," without at that stage knowing any theoretical causal laws governing the behavior of their various configurations.

Conceptual models of this kind may certainly provide suggestions for the development of theory, but if they really appeal to no antecedently known causal relations, it is difficult to imagine that we should have much confidence in any new prediction suggested. Such models would rather be regarded as imaginative devices to be modified and fitted ad hoc to the data. There is no doubt that this is a common mode of scientific reasoning (it is well described in terms of chemical examples by E. F. Caldin in his book *The Structure of Chemistry*). These conceptual models are strongly predictive, since they give new interpretations of theoretical terms into observables which are nonarbitrary in the sense that they are determined by the model itself. But in another sense, the model itself must be regarded as arbitrary, since no further justification can be given for assuming that the world will be like the model. Thus for conceptual models there is no solution of the *logical* problem of analogy, and therefore in what follows we shall restrict ourselves to material analogue models which do satisfy condition (2).

## Models Associated with False Theories

Consider as an example the fluid theory of heat. The fluid model first suggested itself because of some positive analogy between fluid flow and heat conduction. There was already, of course, some known negative analogy, for example, heat fluids seemed to be weightless. This negative analogy did not, however, prevent the fluid model being an acceptable model$_2$ for heat. But subsequent investigation of the neutral analogy showed that other properties of fluids could not be correctly predicated of heat, for example, the heat "fluid" was not conserved. Now at this point a decision regarding the continued acceptability of the model has to rest upon a decision about the importance, relative to the model, of the property of conservation. If conservation is not an "essential" property of fluids, it may be relegated to the negative analogy in the comparison with heat, and the rest of the heat-fluid model₁ retained, as happened with the property of weight. But if conservation is judged to be essenital to a fluid model, *this* negative analogy will be taken to be sufficient to *refute* the heat-fluid model, and the fluid theory will then be said to be false.

The important question clearly is, when is a property of a model essential? No clear-cut answer can be given to this, but various central considerations may be suggested. First, properties which are causally closely related to the known positive analogy in the model are essential. For example, if the causal relations within the positive analogy are mechanical, mechanical properties are essential, but properties such as color, absolute size, etc. may not be. Thus all macroscopic particles have color, but both size and color may be part of their negative analogy with atomic particles without refuting the model. Even some mechanical properties in a mechanical model may be less essential than others. In the case of heat fluid, weightlessness was not sufficient to refute the model, because the conception of mechanical substance implied was that of the "elastic fluid," whose parts exerted mutual repulsive forces but might not be subject to the attractive force of gravity. From this point of view, all matter is subject to the causal relations of central-force mechanics, but not necessarily to the inverse-square law of gravitation. Conservation, on the other hand, *does* seem to be essential to this model, for if conservation is part of the

negative analogy, it is difficult to see what other useful properties of elastic fluids are left in the neutral
analogy. A second consideration determining that a
property is essential, then, is that it is causally so
closely related to the rest of the neutral analogy, that
the whole of this would become part of the negative analogy if the property in question were shown
to be so. Third, it may be suggested that so long as
*some* neutral analogy remains unaffected, the model
may be retained in spite of encroachment of the negative analogy into essential properties, but the li-
cense allowed to a model in this respect will depend
on the availability of alternative models. Thus
Bohr's model of the atom jettisoned some of the essential properties of "particle" and yet remained
acceptable for a time, and the particle and wave
models are still retained in an important sense in
spite of the fact that they, as it were, constitute each
other's negative analogy with the explicandum in essential respects. The major reason why they are retained is surely the extreme difficulty of finding any
satisfactory alternative model.

Models associated with false theories may, then,
satisfy the two conditions stated above and yet they
do not constitute models in the sense required for
prediction. In order to exclude them a third condition is required, which may be stated as follows.

3. The essential properties and causal relations of
the model have not been shown to be part of the
negative analogy between model and explicandum.

Whether properties and relations are "essential" will, however, depend partly on judgments of what is causally essential to the model, and partly on the current availability of alternative models.

### Analogue Machines

In the case of machines (including mechanical, electronic, or even chemical components) which are built in order to simulate the behavior of the explicandum, it may seem that we have systems satisfying conditions (1), (2), and (3), which are yet not suitable candidates for a model$_2$ of the explicandum. Nineteenth-century mechanical ether-models were not intended to reproduce the actual component structure of the ether, and electronic brain-models are not supposed to replicate the biochemical structure of the brain. These cases do not, however, provide real counter-examples to the conditions suggested. They are useful and necessary as predictive models precisely in those cases where the material substance of parts of the analogue is *not essential* to the model, but where the mutual relations of the parts are essential. The material substance therefore constitutes the innocuous negative analogy, whereas the laws of behavior constitute the positive or neutral analogy. As in the previous case, the question of how many of the properties of the analogue-model are essential admits of no definite answer in general, but the relevant considerations will be the same as those already discussed.

## MEANING OF THEORETICAL TERMS

This chapter has so far been concerned wholly with analogies with *observables* in the explicandum, but in conclusion let us look briefly at another use of analogy in connection with scientific models. The analysis of analogy in terms of relations of similarity and causality has been directed to answering questions such as: What is meant by the analogical relation

$$\frac{\text{properties of sound}}{\text{pitch}} :: \frac{\text{observable properties of light}}{\text{color}}?$$

If the arguments of this chapter are accepted, it will be agreed that there is a material, pretheoretic analogy here, and that it is in virtue of this analogy that we use sound as a model for light and make predictions about color *before* we have any theory of color. The suggestion immediately arises, however, that there are also analogical relations in which one term is *unobservable,* that is, is a theoretical term. An example would be:

$$\frac{\text{elastic balls}}{\text{bouncing}} :: \frac{\text{gas molecules}}{\text{pressure}}$$

or as an example from sound and light:

$$\frac{\text{air}}{\text{sound}} :: \frac{\text{ether}}{\text{light}}$$

where "gas molecules" and "ether" are theoretical terms.

It is clearly possible to interpret these last two examples as *formal analogies,* that is to say, terms in the same horizontal row are interpretations of the same symbol or set of symbols of the formal kinetic theory in the first example, or the formal wave theory in the second. This, however, says nothing about the theoretical terms "gas molecules" or "ether" except that they *are* such interpretations—and any other form of words would have done just as well to name the interpretations. But, given the formal analogy, we can also regard these examples as *material analogies* in the sense defined. In this case the vertical causal relations are shown by the position of the terms in the deductive systems of the theories, and the horizontal similarity relations between the *observables* in the lower row are given by an overlap of observable characters as before. Now consider the relation between "air" and "ether" in the second example. "Air" in this analogy must be interpreted as a complex of characters; to say "sound travels in air" is to ascribe an indefinitely long list of characters to air of which some of the relevant ones of this analogy are "air is a chemical substance capable of oscillation having a certain density, a certain elasticity . . . ," and so on. Thus air might be represented by the sum of characters $A_1 \ldots A_n B_1 \ldots B_m D_1 \ldots D_k$. Let us suppose that $B_1 \ldots B_m$ represent the *known positive analogy* between sound and light, including characters associated with wave motion, and $D_1 \ldots D_k$ represent the neutral analogy, including the density, elasticity, and chemical composition of the medium of the waves. Then the theoretical term "ether," corresponding to "air," may be interpreted in one of two ways, either as including the positive and negative analogies only, as $B_1 \ldots B_m C_1 \ldots C_l$, or including also the neutral analogy, as $B_1 \ldots B_m C_1 \ldots C_l D_1 \ldots D_k$. The second interpretation of "ether" represents the analogy between what I have called $\text{model}_2$ (in this case sound) and $\text{model}_1$ (in this case the wave theory of light); the first represents that between $\text{model}_2$ and the known positive analogy between light and sound. It will be noticed that the first alternative introduces no terms not already in the formal analogy between $\text{model}_2$ and the accepted theory, whereas the second alternative introduces also the growing points of the theory. The two interpretations can be illustrated as follows:

| PROJECTED THEORY— $\text{MODEL}_1$ | $\text{MODEL}_2$ | ACCEPTED THEORY |
|---|---|---|
| | (all observables) | |
| light waves | sound waves | light waves |
| intensity | loudness | intensity |
| color | pitch | color |
| ether motion | air motion | ether motion |
| ether density | air density | |
| ether elasticity | air elasticity | |
| ⋮ | ⋮ | |

| ←————————→ | ←————————→ |
|:---:|:---:|
| similarity relations of positive and neutral analogy | similarity relations of positive analogy only |

The difference between the material analogies, containing only observables, which have been previously discussed, and the material analogies containing at least one theoretical term, lies in their use rather than in their nature. In the first case we have been concerned with the use of analogy to infer from three or more given observable terms to another predicted observable; in the second case the scientific use of the analogy is rather to pass from three given observables to the *definition* of a theoretical term, and hence to hypotheses about the theoretical term. The theoretical term may be regarded as a convenient way of summarizing the positive and neutral analogy at any given stage of investigation, and hence of suggesting new, observable predictions by means of the neutral analogy. *Justification* of the postulate of the theoretical term will depend on the success of these predictions, but the *meaning* of the term is clarified by showing how it is partially defined by the characters (the $B$'s) which it shares with the corresponding term in model$_2$.

There need be no conflict between this way of regarding theoretical terms and the more usual account of their meaning as partially defined by their deductive relations with observables. It has already been argued that this "partial definition" is not sufficient, and the account now given supplements it in just the way required. This account depends on the assumption that the identity of formal structure between the model$_2$ and the theory of the explicandum is due to identities between characters (the $B$'s) in one, and corresponding characters in the other. In model$_2$ these characters when combined with the $A$'s may represent observables; in the theory they are combined with the $C$'s and represent theoretical terms or "unobservables." Definition of the theoretical terms as containing the $B$'s is more satisfactory than their partial definition in terms of the observables of the explicandum only. Looked at in this way it might be said that argument from models presupposes identity of characters between model$_2$ and theory in *essential* respects, where "essential" means those respects which are relevant to the causal structure of both model$_2$ and theory. The known differences, or negative analogies, can be regarded as *accidental* to the causal structure. Thus the definition of a theoretical term by means of a model$_2$ is a definition of its essential characters, and if the neutral analogy is included in the definition, as in the second alternative above, this presupposes that the characters in the neutral analogy are also essential rather than accidental. That this may be in fact false, and that the theory will then be false, does not affect our understanding of the *meaning* of the theoretical term.

It may now be asked whether this account of the

meaning of theoretical terms is necessary to the general account of the use of models for prediction. We were able to describe the reasoning which led to such predictions apparently without mentioning the nonobservable terms occurring in the theory of the explicandum. Can we not regard the predictive process as consisting wholly of reasoning by analogy from the observed behavior of the model$_2$ to observable behavior of the explicandum, without going via the theory in either case?[5] Thus, some observed analogies of behavior between sound and light may lead to further predictions about light, without any theory of either sound or light.

This would not, however, be in general a sufficient account of the matter. First, it is the theory of model$_2$ which defines the causal relations of that model, and hence shows what are its essential properties and also what kind of causal relation is involved. As we have seen in several examples, it is not justifiable to pass by analogy from model$_2$ to explicandum in respect either of properties which are not essential to the model or of causal relations of a kind which are not appropriate to model or explicandum. Second, it is model$_2$ which supplies suggestions for extensions of the theory of the explicandum, and in seeing how this theory can yield new predictions in the domain of the explicandum it is often necessary to take account of differences

5. I owe this suggestion to Mr. John Richard Thomson, of King's College, Cambridge.

as well as similarities. This will involve reasoning by analogy about the theoretical terms as well as about analogous observables. Sometimes there may be only a question of numerical constants, as when the scale of $model_2$ is greater than that of the explicandum, and the effect of the scale on the observables has to be calculated in terms of the theories of both $model_2$ and explicandum. Or the difference may be more fundamental, as, for example, in the case of the effect on the velocities of light and sound of passage into a denser medium. The wave theory of sound then has to be generalized to take account of velocities which are diminished instead of increased under these circumstances. As soon as $model_2$ gives way to $model_1$ in the reasoning, by the conscious exclusion of the known negative analogy, it is not sufficient to say that reasoning by analogy consists merely in passing from the observable $model_2$ to the observable explicandum. Third, and finally, if we regard a valid argument by analogy from models as essentially a transfer of causal relations between some characters from one side of the analogy relation to the other, it follows that the interpretation of theoretical terms we have just given is *presupposed* in the argument, even if not explicitly referred to, for if there is a theory about the causal relations in $model_2$, then the same theory holds for the relevant characters in $model_1$, and hence for the explanatory theory being sought.

To summarize the discussion so far: We have

found the distinction between *formal* and *material* analogy to be crucial to the predictive use of scientific models, and in this chapter material analogy has been characterized by two types of dyadic relation, those of *similarity* and *causality*. Analogical arguments from models have been formulated in terms of *characters* which are independently observable but not also experimentally separable. In connection with the justification of analogical argument, a distinction has been made between the *logical* problem of justifying inference from similarity and the *causal* problem of deciding whether the type of vertical relation implied in the analogy is acceptable as causal for either or both of the analogues. Finally, the problem of the meaning of theoretical terms has been elucidated in terms of the analogy relation defined. We now go on to study the logical problem of analogical inference.

# The Logic of Analogy

The logical problem of justification of analogical argument was described in the last chapter as follows:

> An analogue $x$ containing the characters $ABD$ is a model for an explicandum $y$ containing $BC$ but not $A$, where $B$ represents the total known similarity between $x$ and $y$. If $A$ and $B$ together are known to be causally connected to $D$ in the model, are there any rational grounds for expecting or inferring the occurrence of $D$ with $B$ and $C$ in the absence of $A$?

This is a weaker form of argument than is often stated, for in reasoning from scientific models it is not necessary to claim that we can infer with high probability, much less with certainty, that model and explicandum are similar in respects other than those already observed, but merely that, given the choice between a hypothetical explanation based on a model and one which is not, it is *more reasonable* to select the former. The sense of "more reasonable" involved here is what has to be investigated in this chapter.

First, let us distinguish three types of solution to the problem, in increasing order of difficulty.

1. It may be shown merely that, given a choice between a hypothesis based on a model and one

which is not, it is more reasonable to select the former. That is to say, in terms of the symbolism introduced above, it is more reasonable on the given evidence to select the hypothesis $BCD$ than $BCX$, where $X$ is a factor not present in the model and no further information is available.

Or it may be shown that, given two models, one of which has more similarity to the explicandum than the other, it is more reasonable to select the hypothesis based on the former. This may be stated in a weaker and a stronger form:

2. When the set of factors in virtue of which one model is similar to the explicandum *includes* the set in virtue of which the other is similar to the explicandum. That is, given models $A_1B_1D_1$ and $A_2B_1B_2D_2$, and explicandum $B_1B_2C$, containing neither $A_1$ nor $A_2$, it is more reasonable to choose the hypothesis $B_1B_2CD_2$ than $B_1B_2CD_1$, since the similarity characters $B_1B_2$ in the second model include the similarity character $B_1$ in the first model.

3. Or, the solution may enable a comparison to be made between any two models whatever. That is, it may be shown that, given models $A_1B_1D_1$ and $A_2B_2B_3D_2$ with explicandum $B_1B_2B_3C$, it is more reasonable to choose the hypothesis $B_1B_2B_3CD_2$ than $B_1B_2B_3CD_1$, since $B_1B_2B_3C$ is more similar to $A_2B_2B_3D_2$ than to $A_1B_1D_1$. This solution involves not merely the ability to distinguish similarity from dissimilarity, but also to recognize *degrees of similarity,* either comparatively or quantitatively.

The crux of the problem is, of course, the nature of the "rational grounds" which can be adduced in favor of the argument from analogy. Since the problem is one of choice between hypotheses, we shall proceed by surveying some of the suggestions that have been made about the criteria according to which such choices are made. Traditionally, analogy has been regarded as a species of inductive reasoning, so that the problem of justification of analogical argument is seen in terms of strength of *inductive support*. Various accounts of choice between hypotheses by assigning to them *probability* on the basis of inductive evidence remain within this traditional framework and indeed have sometimes been seen as attempts to justify inductive inference itself in terms of noninductive assumptions, although this view of inductive probability has now been largely abandoned. Dissatisfaction with it, and with all forms of "solution" of the problem of induction, has more recently led to exploration of other kinds of criteria of choice between hypotheses, principally in terms of their *falsifiability* or their *simplicity*. We shall examine the problem of analogy as a problem of choice between hypotheses from four points of view: (1) choice is made according to *strength of inductive support;* (2) probability values are assigned to hypotheses on the basis of evidence, and choice is made of the most *probable;* (3) choice is made of the most *falsifiable* hypothesis; (4) the *simplest* hypothesis is chosen.

## INDUCTIVE SUPPORT

Any argument which concludes that certain connections are present in new instances in virtue of their presence in available evidence may be said to rely on inductive support. The analogical argument from the evidence of a model $ABD$ to the hypothesis that $BC$, which does not contain $A$ does contain $D$, has inductive support, since it is assumed that the only evidence available about the explicandum comes from the presence of $B$ in the model, and thus the only conclusion that could be based on the evidence is that $BC$ contains $D$. Thus problem (1) is solved by this method by remarking that the hypothesis based on the model is the only one having inductive support.

To investigate the problem in more detail, take the simple special case where the causal connection between $AB$ and $D$ is the universal law "All $AB$'s are $D$," and we are concerned to choose only between hypotheses which are also universal laws. Given explicandum $BC$ and model $ABD$, the evidence is "All $AB$'s are $D$." There are three possible hypotheses inductively supported by this evidence, namely: "All $A$'s are $D$ and All $B$'s are $D$"; "All $A$'s are $D$"; "All $B$'s are $D$." Of these only "All $B$'s are $D$" is relevant to the explicandum containing $B$ and $C$ but not $A$; thus this law has inductive support, and it leads to the only hypothesis concerning the explicandum which has such support, namely "All

$BC$'s are $D$." Notice that there is no assumption here that the characters are causally additive: it might be the case that $A$ and $B$ occur with $D$ when conjoined, but never when occurring separately or with other characters such as $C$. If this is known to be the case, *no* hypothesis about $BC$ can be given inductive support by this evidence. But if it is not known to be the case, then "All $BC$'s are $D$" is the only hypothesis with inductive support in the field.

Now suppose, as envisaged in problem (2), that two models, $A_1B_1D_1$ and $A_2B_1B_2D_2$, are introduced, and that the explicandum is $B_1B_2C$. The first model suggests the hypothesis "All $B_1$'s are $D_1$" by the same argument as before, but the evidence of the second model now *refutes* this hypothesis drawn from the first model, because the second model does not contain $D_1$. It therefore appears to weaken, although it does not refute, the hypothesis "All $B_1B_2C$'s are $D_1$." If, however, we had started with the second model, the hypothesis "All $B_1B_2$'s are $D_2$" would have been derived from it, and this model would not have been refuted by introduction of the model $A_1B_1D_1$. We should therefore regard the hypothesis "All $B_1B_2C$'s are $D_2$" as unaffected, and this suggests that on the basis of the two models, it is more reasonable to choose "All $B_1B_2C$'s are $D_2$" than its rival "All $B_1B_2C$'s are $D_1$." Thus some rational grounds can be given for the solution of problem (2) by inductive support, although only by a somewhat dubious stretching of the inductive criterion.

No solution of this kind can, however, be suggested for problem (3). In this case the model $A_1B_1D_1$ suggests the hypothesis "All $B_1$'s are $D_1$," and this is unaffected by the second model $A_2B_2B_3D_2$, and similarly the hypothesis "All $B_2B_3$'s are $D_2$" drawn from the second model is unaffected by the model $A_1B_1D_1$. On the other hand, this result seems in conflict with common sense, for we should generally have more confidence in a hypothesis based on a model very similar to the explicandum than on a model much less similar. This common-sense assumption seems to depend on an unformulated notion of the higher probability of association of $D_2$ with $B_2B_3$ than of $D_1$ with $B_1$, given the models, and brings us to the second suggestion for a criterion of choice between hypotheses, namely their probability on the basis of evidence.

## PROBABILITY OF HYPOTHESES

Problem (3) would be solved if we were able to argue that since $A_2B_2B_3D_2$ is *more similar* to $B_1B_2B_3C$ than is $A_1B_1D_1$, it is *more probable* that $B_1B_2B_3C$ also contains $D_2$ than that it contains $D_1$. Such an argument presupposes that the characters $B_1$, $B_2$, $B_3$ are somehow of equal weight and that the probability of a causal connection existing between any group of them and another factor is proportional to the number in the group. Investigation and attempted justification of assumptions such as these form the subject-matter of *confirmation theory* as developed by, among others, Keynes, Broad, Carnap, and Von Wright. Such theories encounter great difficulties, both technical and philosophical, and I shall not attempt anything like a general account of them here. But I shall try to indicate some of the difficulties and assumptions involved in treating analogical argument by methods of this kind.

Let us begin by considering problem (1), given model $ABD$ and explicandum $BC$ not containing $A$. We have to show that the explicandum is more likely to contain $D$ than any other character not in the evidence, say $X$. Let us suppose that the universe constituting the domain of the argument contains $N$ characters which are associated in groups, each containing three different characters, and that the total number, $M$, of different groups in the universe is much less than the total number of possible combinations of the $N$ characters in groups of three. That is to say, the universe is such that groups containing certain combinations of characters are excluded, but there may be any number of instances of the same group if this group does occur. Suppose, further, that the particular selection of $M$ groups is unknown, but that any group of three characters is a priori as likely to occur in it as any other, that any group is as likely as any other to be selected as evidence out of the universe, and that such selections are independent. Let us call this the *chance universe*.

Now it is clearly some such universe that we are presupposing when we intuitively argue from similarity in a number of characters to similarity in others, that is to say, we assume that characters occur in a limited number of different groups.[1] But so far, this definition of the universe is not strong enough even to allow us to deal with problem (1). For if any group of three characters is as likely to occur as any other, the evidence of the model, that the group $ABD$ occurs, can have no effect on the chance of $BC$ containing $D$ rather than $X$. The chances of $BCD$ and $BCX$ remain the same, and remain at the value assumed a priori. Thus no analogy argument of the kind we have defined is justified in the chance universe.

But it should be noticed that if we are concerned with a purely *inductive* argument from say $ABD$ to $ABx$, where $x$ is an unknown third character, the probability of $x = D$ in a chance universe *is* greater than that of $x = X$. Here we know that $ABD$ is one of the $M$ groups in the universe, hence the probability that $x = D$ is $1/M$. But $X$ is one of $N - 3$ other characters, all equally likely to appear, hence the probability that $x = X$ is

$$\frac{1}{N-3}\left(1 - \frac{1}{M}\right)$$

and since $N$ is very much greater than $M$, this is very much less than $1/M$. In this inductive argument it is the possibility that the explicandum is an in-

---

1. This is a version of Keynes' "Principle of Limited Independent Variety."

stance of the *same* group as the model that gives a greater probability for $x = D$ than for $x = X$. But in a true analogy argument, that possibility is excluded by the conditions of the problem, and so stronger-than-chance assumptions about the universe are required if the argument is to be justified. One might put this by saying that inductive argument is possible in a "Humean" chance universe, where causal connection is merely frequency of chance co-occurrence, but for analogical argument a universe of stronger causal connections is required.[2]

Von Wright suggests that the stronger causal connection is provided by the assumption of laws asserting that certain characters or sets of characters are necessary or sufficient conditions of other sets of characters. Such laws are to be interpreted as connections between sets of characters, which can be carried over from one group to another, in particular from groups known in the evidence to groups as yet unknown. The function of the model $ABD$ is then to suggest as a hypothesis that there is a law "All $B$'s are $D$" which, if the hypothesis is true, gives for the explicandum $BCD$.

Difficulties arise, however, as soon as we attempt to assign to the law "All $B$'s are $D$" a probability which increases with the amount of confirming evidence. There is such a prior probability in the

2. Carnap's $c^*$ universe is a chance universe in this sense, and the form of analogical argument which he describes is not what has been defined here, but the same as the inductive argument in this paragraph (*Logical Foundations of Probability*, p. 569).

chance universe—it is the probability that the $M$ groups are such that every one that contains $B$ also contains $D$. This has a chance value before the collection of evidence, and this value increases with all observed instances of $B$'s which are $D$, provided no $B$'s which are not $D$ are observed. In the present case, it increases with the evidence that one of the groups is $ABD$. But we have already seen that this evidence can have no effect on the probability that $BC$ is $D$, and indeed we find that although the probability that $BC$ is $D$ as an instance of "All $B$'s are $D$" is increased, its probability as an instance of other laws whose probabilities are also affected by the evidence of the model is either increased or decreased in such a way that the resulting probability remains at its chance value. Thus if the argument from analogy is to be justified, the prior probability of the law "All $B$'s are $D$" must have some value other than that given to it by frequency of co-occurrence in the chance universe.

Supposing for the moment that it has such a probability, let us see how far the probability method will take us with the analogy problems. Suppose, for example, that experience predisposes us to expect that there will be laws of the form "All $B$'s are $D$" and that we are therefore prepared to assign to these laws a prior probability greater than chance. Then it can be shown that, provided this prior probability is *greater than some number greater than zero* (a probability greater than zero but tending to zero as a limit will not do), then the posterior probability of the law increases with each new instance which is not maximally probable relative to previous evidence. Von Wright applies this theorem to an argument from analogy as follows. Suppose a set of characters $AB_1 \ldots B_m$ (the model) is known to be a sufficient condition for $D$, then the probability of $B_1 \ldots B_m$ being or containing a sufficient condition for $D$ is greater than that of $B_1 \ldots B_{m-1}$ containing such a sufficient condition. In other words, the more similar the explicandum is to the model, the more likely it is also to contain the character $D$. This does not yet take account of the *difference* between model and explicandum, but a slight modification of the proof enables it to do so, and we can then go on to suggest a solution to problem (1).

Denote the causal law "All $B$'s are $D$" by the proposition $(B \to D)$. (Strictly, $(x) \, B \, (x) \supset D \, (x)$ or, "For all $x$, if $x$ is $B$ then $x$ is $D$," but we can abbreviate this without loss of rigor.) The model is then represented by the proposition, $m$, where

$$m \quad (AB \to D).$$
$$df$$

Denote the probability of the law on prior evidence $e$ by

$$P[\,(B \to D)/e\,]$$

Since the proposition $(B \to D)$ is logically equivalent to $(BA \to D) \, \& \, (B \sim A \to D)$, where $\sim A$ is not -$A$, we can write

$$P[\,(B \to D)/e\,] = P[\,(BA \to D) \ \& \ (B \sim A \to D)]/e$$
$$= P[\,(AB \to D)/e].$$
$$P[(B \sim A \to D)/e \ \& \ (AB \to D)]$$

by the multiplication rule for probabilities.

But $P[\,(B \sim A \to D)/e \ \& \ (AB \to D)]$ is just the posterior probability we require that $B$ is a sufficient condition of $D$ in the absence of $A$, on the prior evidence plus the evidence of the model. If $P[\,(B \to D)/e\,]$ is finite, and $P[\,(AB \to D)/e\,]$ is less than unity, then we have

$$P[\,(B \sim A \to D)/e \ \& \ m\,] > P[\,(B \to D)/e\,]$$

This means that the evidence of the model increases the probability that the explicandum contains $D$ above its prior value. It does not, however, tell us how the hypothesis $BC \to D$ for the explicandum compares with the hypothesis $BC \to X$ unless we make further assumptions. A set of assumptions which would enable problem (1) to be solved would be the following. Suppose the only rival hypothesis is $C \to X$ (that is, the hypothesis that if $B$ alone is not a sufficient condition for the third character then $C$ is). Suppose further that the prior probabilities $P[\,(B \to D)/e\,]$ and $P[\,(C \to X)/e\,]$ are equal and that the probability of $C \to X$ is not increased by the evidence of the model. We then have the result

$$P[\,(B \sim A \to D)/e \ \& \ m\,] > P[\,(C \to X)/e \ \& \ m].$$

In words, the probability that $BC$ will be sufficient for $D$, given the model $m$, is greater than the probability that $BC$ will be sufficient for any factor $X$ not in the evidence, provided the following conditions are satisfied:

(a) $P[\,(B \to D)/e\,] \geqslant_{\epsilon} > 0.$

(b) $P[\,(AB \to D)/e\,] < 1.$

(c) If $BC$ is a sufficient condition for a third character, then either $B$ is its sufficient condition, or $C$ is its sufficient condition.

(d) $P[\,(C \to X)/e\,] = P[\,(B \to D)/e\,].$

(e) $P[\,(C \to X)/e \,\&\, m\,] \leqslant P[\,(C \to X)/e\,].$

Clearly this method adds nothing to the justification already given from inductive support, for what it gains in precision it loses in the number and obscurity of the assumptions that have to be made even to provide a solution to problem (1). None of these five conditions, except perhaps (b), are of a kind that one would be more willing to accept without further justification than the analogical argument itself. And it is very hard to see what further justification could be provided. A confirmation theory which systematized a number of diverse methods of inductive and statistical reasoning in terms of a few simple postulates might indeed be said to give a justification for the methods, even if its postulates were not further justifiable, just as the theory of gravitation may be said to justify a number of diverse laws of mechanics, even though there is no further explanation of the theory itself. But it is not clear that even Carnap's system provides such a self-justifying confirmation theory, and in any case we have seen that since it assumes a chance universe this system cannot be used to justify analogical inference as understood here. It therefore seems very doubtful whether any system could be found which would justify analogical argument and be acceptable in the sense of being simpler or resting on more plausible assumptions than the argument itself.

It must be concluded also that the probability method gives no help with problems (2) or (3). It would be quite possible to list the further assumptions which would be required to solve the problems by this method, but there would be little point in doing so, since such a list would do no more than restate the problems in a different form. Since the probability method is the only potentially quantitative method of dealing with analogy, and since even this method fails to solve problems (2) and (3), it may be as well at this point to pause and consider whether it is reasonable to expect *any* solution of these two problems in connection with arguments from models. It does certainly seem reasonable to assume that when a model is *very similar* to the explicandum, it should be preferred to any model which is not very similar. This is a special case of problem (2) or (3), and any method which does not give an account of it seems intuitively inadequate. I shall return to it presently. But meanwhile, in regard to the general form of the problems, the reasonableness of expecting a solution seems more doubtful.

It is difficult to imagine a realistic situation of choice between models where the choice obviously hangs on a judgment about which model is *more similar* to the explicandum. If we consider that even great similarity still implies at least one character different, and if we have no evidence other than the models and no means of weighting the importance of characters, it seems no more reasonable to ignore the differences than the similarities. In any case a decision seldom has to be made simply on a judgment of degrees of similarity. In the first place, comparison of such "degrees" is all but impossible in any practical case (think of the corpuscular and wave theories of light before any of the crucial experiments had been performed), and, in the second place, other considerations will often enter at this stage. We may, for example, take into account previous successes of models of the same kind, and how far one or other model fits into the types of theory already accepted. Again, the formal simplicity of the *theories* of the two competing models (for example, particle mechanics and wave mechanics) is obviously relevant here. It has been argued before that simplicity of the formal theory is not a *sufficient* criterion of choice between hypotheses, since the formalism needs interpretation if it is to be strongly predictive, but it may still be a criterion supplementing the other choice criteria when more than one model is involved. These other criteria give grounds for choosing an interpretation based on *some* model; the choice *between* models may then be made in terms of formal simplicity or other formal characteristics of their respective theories.

But what, on the other hand, can we say about a situation in which there is very great similarity in the case of one model and only moderate similarity in the case of another? If we consider as examples two different planets with very similar properties or two chemical compounds with very similar structures, it seems likely that in cases such as these it is not only the similarities which cause us to have confidence in arguing from one analogue to the other, but also the *apparent irrelevance of the differences*. In other words, cases of great similarity are assimilated to cases of inductive argument by neglecting their differences. Indeed, we have already seen that the notion of "degrees of similarity" is a dubious one, and it may be that we only make the judgment "very similar" when we also presuppose that the differences are such that they can be neglected in relation to arguments concerning the similarities. Such a judgment will already depend on inductive experience, for example, that the size of planets is irrelevant to the laws satisfied by their mechanical and chemical properties. Thus, when faced with two models to choose from, to choose one because it is "very similar" to the explicandum is to assume that this one can be treated as an *inductive* instance of a generalization of which the explicandum is another instance, and in this case, even in a chance universe this generalization will have a greater-than-chance probability on the evidence, whereas hypotheses based only on *analogy* with any other model will have only chance probability in the chance universe.

The results of this investigation of probability of hypotheses as a possible justification of argument from analogy have been largely negative. One of the negative results has, however, some importance, that is, the discovery that no inductive support will justify argument from analogy in a chance universe. We therefore have to add to the considerations regarding inductive evidence in the previous section the requirement that the domain of the argument is not a chance universe, for if it is, *none* of the hypotheses suggested by the model is relevant to the explicandum. But inductive justification does not depend on our *knowing* that this requirement is satisfied, because we certainly do not know of any of the domains of application of scientific models that they *are* chance universes, therefore it is still reasonable to act on the assumption that they are *not*, and this is the only assumption that gives any principle of selection between hypotheses based on inductive support. The alternative is not a different principle of selection, but no principle at all. Therefore, *if the method of inductive support is accepted at all* the argument from models is justified by it.

The ungarnished notion of inductive support, however, is not universally accepted as giving any reasonable grounds for inference to hypotheses. Popper, in particular, has wholly rejected all methods of inferring from particular to general or from particular to new particular and has claimed to base his logic of science instead on the wholly deductive notion of falsifiability, which we consider next.

## FALSIFIABILITY

According to Popper's view, typical scientific hypotheses are universal statements, that is to say, of the form "All $Y$'s are $Z$," and are therefore falsified by one contrary instance. It is this characteristic of falsifiability that makes them scientific, and not any inductive support or any degree of probability calculated from the evidence. Thus the main criterion of choice between hypotheses discussed by Popper is in terms of "degrees of falsifiability." The prescription is: Choose that hypothesis which has not yet been falsified but which "says more" about the as yet unobserved empirical facts; for this is the hypothesis that will be refuted more quickly if it is false. For example, "All heavenly bodies move in circles" is more general and hence says more than "All planets move in circles"; it therefore gives more opportunities for test and will be refuted quicker if it is false.

Generally, according to this criterion, a hypothesis $H_1$ will be chosen in preference to $H_2$ if all instances that would refute $H_2$ would also refute $H_1$, and if in addition other instances would refute $H_1$ which would leave $H_2$ unaffected. Popper expresses this by saying that the set of *potential falsifiers* of $H_1$ includes and is larger than the set of potential falsifiers of $H_2$.

The criterion is open to several objections, of which two are particularly relevant to its applicability to scientific models. First, it clearly does not reproduce the normal habits of scientists in cases where it would require choice of a more general hypothesis in preference to one which is in some obvious sense simpler or better confirmed. Goodman points this out by means of an example of which an English equivalent is the following:

$H_1$: "All oaks, except those in Cambridge, are deciduous."

$H_2$: "All oaks are deciduous."

$H_3$: "All oaks, and all beeches in Cambridge, are deciduous."

The evidence is assumed to consist of deciduous oaks in places other than Cambridge. Here $H_2$ would generally be preferred to $H_1$ on grounds of its greater generality *and* simplicity, and hence falsifiability, but $H_2$ would usually also be preferred to $H_3$ although it is less general and falsifiable, because it is simpler and better confirmed by the evidence.

A second difficulty is that in many cases hypotheses will not be comparable by the falsifiability criterion, because the potential falsifiers of one do not include those of the other. It is then impossible to decide which "says more about" the world, because there is no way of "weighting" the potential falsifiers in the two cases. Suppose, for example, that $H_1$ would be refuted by sets of observations $O_1$ and $O_2$, and $H_2$ would be refuted by sets of observations $O_2$ and $O_3$. Without a measure of the atomic statements in $O_1$ and $O_3$ it is impossible to compare the falsifiability of $H_1$ and $H_2$.

It should be pointed out that Popper himself is not directly concerned with the question of *choice* between hypotheses, but rather what makes a hypothesis *scientific* (as opposed to logical or metaphysical), and he gives no clear answer to these two objections. In particular, he does not wish to propose a measure of atomic statements such as would make his falsifiability criterion a general criterion of choice between any hypotheses. But he does in places admit a further requirement for a good hypothesis, namely, that it shall have "stood up to tests" designed to falsify it if it is in fact false. This criterion is called by Popper *corroboration*. It is not easy to see how the results of applying this criterion can differ from those of the criterion of inductive support, but the reasons underlying its introduction by Popper cannot be inductive, since he utterly rejects induction as a source of logical support in any sense. For Popper, corroboration cannot add to the likelihood that a hypothesis will be *true*; what, then, is its place in his system? It is impossible to find a clear answer to this in Popper's writings, but certain passages indicate that he has two considerations in mind. First, he thinks that we naturally (or "by habit" as Hume said) find ourselves generalizing from the data we have, and therefore any hypothesis that is likely to present itself for consideration will already be corroborated by some data. This is of course, for Popper, a wholly "psychological" remark and not at all concerned with justification, but it may be taken as a sufficient basis for the assumption, which we shall presently make, that we can only sensibly ask about criteria of choice between hypotheses in terms of falsifiability when the hypotheses are in the first place relevant to some data already experienced. Popper does not wish to suggest that scientists are presented with unreal choices between an infinity of possible hypotheses about anything whatever, for in that case construction of highly falsifiable hypotheses would be only too easy for those with sufficiently bizarre imaginations.

Second, Popper conceives of science as a "game" which is essentially a continuing search for more and more general hypotheses which are as yet unfalsified. Now although this is a never-ending process and we never reach universal "truth," yet it is possible to say that a better corroborated hypothesis has gone further along this road, at least in regard to particular instances, than one that is worse corroborated or not corroborated at all. The justification of falsifiability as a criterion is the quasi-pragmatic one that it allows the game to go on as rapidly as possible, since the most falsifiable hypothesis is the one that is eliminated quickest if it is false. Analogously it could be argued, although Popper seems not to have explicitly done so, that the pragmatic justification of corroboration is that without it there would be no game at all, for if some hypotheses were not corroborated, at least in limited fields of application, there would be no point in trying to generalize them over wider and wider domains.

This is not the place to pursue any further the objections to corroboration in Popper's system. Let us instead consider how far a falsifiability criterion, with or without corroboration, will take us with the problem of analogical argument.

Consider first the process of generalizing from "$Y_1$, $Y_2$, $Y_3$ are $Z$" to "All $Y$'s are $Z$." We shall not assume that there is any "inductive argument" here, but only that we have to choose between various hypotheses, given the data, and that the hypotheses that arise for consideration ("psychologically," if we accept Popper's standpoint) are at least hypotheses about the terms in the data. If we confine ourselves to universal and existential forms, there are four logically possible hypotheses:

$H_1$: "All $Y$'s are $Z$."

$H_2$: "Not all $Y$'s are $Z$" or "There is a $Y$ which is not $Z$."

$H_3$: "All $Y$'s are $X$," where $X$ implies not-$Z$.

$H_4$: "All $Y$'s except $Y_1$, $Y_2$, $Y_3$ are $X$," where $X$ implies not-$Z$.

The falsifiability criterion disposes at once of $H_2$ and $H_3$. Given the data, $H_3$ has been falsified. $H_2$, on the other hand, is *not falsifiable,* because, assuming (as Popper does for all scientific laws) that we are dealing with an infinite class, no finite evidence could show $H_2$ to be *false,* just as no finite evidence could show $H_1$ to be *true.* There remains $H_4$. This might be said to be unacceptable as a scientific hypothesis in any case, because, although universal in form, it mentions particular instances which depend on what happens to have been observed. It is a typical example of what Popper calls ad hoc hypothesis, tailored for some ulterior reason to the evidence. Also, it has stood up to no tests, because no tests have been made on the class of things mentioned in the law, namely the $Y$'s other than $Y_1$, $Y_2$, $Y_3$. Thus in conformity with what appear to be Popper's intentions, we have to reject $H_4$. Since there are no other universal hypotheses relevant to the terms $Y$ and $Z$, we can conclude that a falsifiability criterion accounts for ordinary generalization. This, of course, is not surprising, because "All $Y$'s are $Z$" is Popper's paradigm of a scientific law, from which he derives most of his arguments in favor of the falsifiability criterion itself.

This somewhat tedious method of dealing with generalizations does, however, suggest how we should try to apply the falsifiability criterion to arguments from models. If the model is "All $AB$'s are $D$" as before and we again confine ourselves to universal and existential forms, we have the following competing hypotheses about the explicandum $BC$:

$T_1$: "All $B$'s are $D$."

$T_2$: "All $BC$'s are $D$." This is less testable than $T_1$.

$T_3$: "Not all $B$'s are $D$." This is unfalsifiable.

$T_4$: "All $B$'s are $X$," where $X$ implies not-$D$. This is false.

$T_5$: "All $B$'s except $AB$'s are $X$." This is less testable than $T_1$.

$T_6$: "All $B$'s except observed $AB$'s are $X$." This is not an acceptable form of hypothesis and is in any case less corroborated than $T_1$.

$T_7$: "All $BC$'s are $X$." This is less falsifiable than $T_1$.

$T_8$: "All $C$'s are $X$." The falsifiability of this is not comparable with that of $T_1$.

According to the falsifiability criterion, then $T_1$ will be preferred to any of $T_2$ to $T_7$, but no choice is possible on these grounds between $T_1$ and $T_8$. If we introduce corroboration, however, $T_8$ is clearly not corroborated by the data, while $T_1$ is corroborated. Thus, if we are prepared to accept corroboration as a criterion, a hypothesis based on a model will be preferred to one that is not, but falsifiability alone will not enable us to make this choice.

The results for problems (2) and (3) are less satisfactory. In problem (2) we have two models, one more similar to the explicandum than the other:

| MODELS | EXPLICANDUM |
|--------|-------------|
| (a) $A_1B_1D_1$ | |
| (b) $A_2B_1B_2D_2$ | $B_1B_2C\ldots$ |

The question is, is it more reasonable to conclude that the explicandum contains $D_2$ than that it contains $D_1$? If we adopt the method of listing all possible and relevant hypotheses and eliminating those which are false, unfalsifiable, or not of maximum falsifiability, we are left with hypotheses which are incomparable on both falsifiability and corroboration criteria, and of which some choose model (b) and others model (a). Thus these combined criteria give no justification for our intuitive choice of model (b). Moreover, the attempt to solve problem (3) by similar methods also leads to the same conclusion. The situation may be compared with that for the criterion of inductive support. There also it was concluded that problem (3) is insoluble, but some support was given to the choice of model (b) in problem (2) by noticing that the evidence provided by model (b) somewhat undermines that provided by model (a). Falsifiability fails to give even this much comfort to the choice of model (b).

## SIMPLICITY

The fourth commonly suggested criterion of choice between hypotheses is simplicity. Many different senses can be given to this, but there is one which is immediately relevant to the choice between the hypotheses $T_1$ to $T_8$ listed in the last section in connection with problem (1). If we eliminate $T_3$ on the grounds that any criterion should require a hypothesis at least to be falsifiable, and $T_4$ on the grounds that no hypothesis should be known to be false, we can compare the remaining hypotheses by means of an obvious criterion of simplicity, namely, by counting the number of characters involved. $T_1$, $T_2$, $T_7$ and $T_8$ are simplest on this criterion, since they each contain two characters, but $T_7$ and $T_8$ both introduce a character $X$ which is not in the evidence and could therefore be eliminated as less simple than $T_1$ or $T_2$ on this ground. We are left with $T_1$ and $T_2$, either of which is a hypothesis about the explicandum derived from the model $ABD$. Hence this sense of simplicity justifies the choice of a hypothesis based on a model.

But again we cannot go on to use this criterion to solve problems (2) and (3). This is because hypotheses which choose model (a) rather than (b) cannot be eliminated on the grounds that they introduce a character extraneous to the evidence, for they introduce only $D_1$, which is in the evidence. Thus, for example, "All $C$'s are $D_1$" will be as simple as "All $B_2$'s are $D_2$." We must conclude that the suggestion made in connection with probability methods that problems (2) and (3) may after all be insoluble is confirmed by this failure to solve them by any of the other conventional criteria of choice.

Let us therefore confine our attention to problem
(1). We have seen that a hypothesis based on a
model is preferable to one which is not on grounds
of inductive support, falsifiability-plus-corrobora-
tion, and simplicity. We shall neglect the solution
given by the probability method, since this is greatly
weakened by the number of doubtful assumptions
required, and adds little to the general inductive criterion. It is, of course, not surprising that since we
have taken the model to be the sole datum in relation to the choice of hypotheses, we should have got
a positive answer to the logical problem by using
criteria which appeal to *data,* namely, induction and
corroboration. The case of simplicity is somewhat
different, for here we appeal to a principle of economy or unity of nature—the preference for a hypothesis which implies as few deviations as possible from
what we already know to exist. This use of a simplicity criterion might be said to be equivalent to the
assumption that natural phenomena exhibit various
forms of an underlying single reality, for example,
mechanism, or electromagnetic field, or whatever
current physics takes to be its fundamental model.
Argument from models can then be seen as the consequence of a general assumption variously described
by saying that all sciences can be reduced to a fundamental science or that there are primary and secondary qualities, of which the secondary are dependent
on, and can be explained in terms of, the primary.
Then, if the observed similarities between analogous

phenomena are similarities in what are taken to be primary qualities, they can indeed be regarded as the *essential* characters from which analogical argument can proceed, and the observed differences of secondary qualities can be regarded as *accidental,* not affecting the inference from causal relations in one analogue to similar causal relations in the other.

It may be objected, of course, that the argument from models understood in this way unduly restricts the *novelty* of theories which have model-interpretations. There is force in this objection, for it is true that novel kinds of theory may be formal or conceptual, and thus may not satisfy the conditions for material analogy which have been assumed in this analysis. In this case they may function as *correlations* of existing data rather than as predictive theories. It is not claimed here that the argument from models by any means exhausts the ways in which hypotheses are constructed and justified, and the answer to the question with which we began, are models logically essential to scientific theories? must be No in general, if by "models" is meant material analogues. But if theories are to conform to certain strong requirements which have usually been demanded of them, then material analogues do become essential. Our discussion has presupposed two such requirements: (a) strong falsifiability or predictive power, that is to say, power to predict relations between *new* observation predicates; (b) some kind of justification in terms of usual choice-criteria for selecting theories which depend on the models required by (a).

The argument for models can be made to depend on requirement (a) alone if it is agreed that to interpret a theory by means of some model in itself gives the theory nonarbitrary predictive power, which it would not have by means of merely ad hoc interpretations of theoretical statements into observation statements. This requirement is satisfied by conceptual models for which no further causal justification is sought. Requirement (b) introduces such further justifications and implies that the model-explicandum relation is one of material analogy with known causal relations between the terms of the model.

In summary, three kinds of theories have been distinguished in terms of their predictive power:

1. *Formal theories* which are only weakly predictive.

2. *Conceptual models* which are strongly predictive but not justified by further choice-criteria.

3. *Material analogue-models* which are both strongly predictive and justified by choice-criteria which appeal to the models as empirical data.

Which kind of theory does, or ought to, predominate at various stages of the development of science is a question which can be settled only in particular scientific contexts.

# Aristotle's Logic of Analogy[1]

There are two different areas in which the problem of analogy chiefly arises in current philosophical literature: (1) the nature and justification of analogical argument in science; (2) the question of analogical predication and perhaps analogical argument in metaphysics and theology.

The latter discussion occurs most usually in neo-Thomist contexts, and there it is usual to distinguish (1) from (2) completely and to suggest that (1) raises no problems, or at least no metaphysical problems. Philosophers of science who concern themselves with (1), on the other hand, find discussion of (2), to say the least, obscure, and tend to regard it as irrelevant to their problems. I believe that the whole question would benefit from a fresh examination, particularly in the light of Aristotle's references to both, because I cannot agree that the first raises no important philosophical issues and because it is worth considering whether Aristotle was right, as against his scholastic successors, in clearly implying a close connection between the two (1-7).[2]

I shall attempt to establish three points:

1. An earlier version of this paper was read at a meeting of the B Club at Cambridge on March 11, 1963. I am indebted to those who commented on it there.
2. Numbers in parentheses refer to literature listed in the Bibliography at the end of this volume.

*First,* that at least one sense of what Aristotle called analogy is what is used and called by that name in modern scientific argument, and that his analysis throws some light on this.

*Second,* that there is an essential continuity between Aristotle's "scientific" and "metaphysical" analogies, but that in metaphysical analogy he is forced to introduce it as an irreducible "third way" between univocity and equivocity, which seems not to be required in scientific analogy.

*Third,* that the way forward is to question, not the notion of analogy, but the notion of univocity, and that both scientific arguments and ordinary language employ analogy as the normal and not the exceptional case.

## SCIENTIFIC ANALOGY

Aristotle's use of "analogy" depends in the first place on his notion of classification of particulars into species and genera. It is easiest, therefore, to start by considering analogy in the biological context of analogies of structure and function between animal species.

In the *Posterior Analytics* (97 b), Aristotle explains how to define a genus: first, observe specifically identical individuals and determine the properties they have in common. Repeat this with sets of individuals of different species, selecting their common properties, and so on until a single formula is reached, depending on a single common character.

This defines the genus. If more than one character is reached by this method and these have nothing further in common, the definiendum is not one thing, but is being used equivocally. For example, pride is either intolerance of insult or equanimity, and these have nothing further in common, hence pride is used equivocally in these two senses. Also, "like" applied to shapes means equality of ratios or sides, but applied to colors it means identity of the act of perceiving them, and these have nothing in common; hence "like" is here used equivocally. This means that nothing can be in more than one genus, and that all differentiae that divide a genus into species are peculiar to the genus, as for example "rational" is peculiar to the genus "animal" and is sufficient by itself to define "man." If the differentiae were not peculiar to one genus they would produce another genus, for example, of "rational beings" including some animals and some nonanimals, but no species such as "rational beings" can be in more than one genus.

In some cases, Aristotle goes on to remark, the properties in common between species do not have a common name, as with the "squid's pounce," "fish's spine," and "animal's bone," but "these possess common properties as if there were a single osseous nature" (98 a). These properties are said to be selected "by analogy." They presumably assist in the definition of the genus "vertebrates," so that here, instead of defining a genus by the common property

*A* identically named in, say, species *AB* and species *AC*, we now define it by the "analogous" properties *A* and *A'* in *AB* and *A'C*.

There are several points to make about this example. First, it seems to depend on the apparently accidental and comparatively trivial fact that there happens to be no word in the Greek language to express what is seen to be in common between the instances. The point is, however, clearly not one merely about language, for Aristotle immediately coins an appropriate phrase, namely "osseous nature," to fill *that* gap. In this example he wishes rather to direct attention to the process of selecting the common properties. This is what is done "by analogy," and it is *in virtue of* the analogy that a common name can be coined. We shall see later that from Aristotle's own point of view, this is a comparatively trivial example of selection by analogy, although the reference to language does have an importance he failed to exploit.

Second, why are the properties said to be "analogous"? The Greek *analogia* is the word used for mathematical proportion, and elsewhere Aristotle makes it clear that he sometimes has this sense in mind. For example, in the *Poetics* he speaks of metaphors as being based on analogy when the relation *B* is to *A* as *D* is to *C* exists—his cup is to Dionysius as his shield is to Ares, so that for "cup" we may say metaphorically "shield of Dionysius" (1457a). By comparison the four-term relation in the biological

example is "spine is to fish as bone is to animal."
In the *Historia Animaium* this relation is explained
in more detail and with further examples. There it
is said that animals whose parts are identical in form
belong to the same species; those whose parts are
identical except for excess or defect of accidents (as
color, shape, hardness, number of feathers, etc.) are
of the same genus; and others are the same "only in
the way of analogy, as for instance bone is only analogous to fish-bone, nail to hoof, hand to claw, and
scale to feather; for what the feather is in a bird, the
scale is in a fish" (486 b).

If we consider these examples, it seems there are
two senses in which the terms are said to be "analogous": (1) when there are *properties in common*
between parts of the members of different species;
for example, spine and bone share an "osseous nature"; (2) when there is similarity in the *relation*
of the parts to the whole in each species; for example, cup *is the symbol of* Dionysius as shield is of
Ares and, more typically, hand and claw, scale and
feather, wings and fins, and so on, have similar structural positions or functions in relation to their respective organisms. Sometimes, perhaps usually,
both senses of analogy apply to the same example.
Where Aristotle is talking about definition of genera
by means of analogously common properties, it seems
that he is referring to the first sense only, for the differentiae are properties, not relations. But the biological examples mentioned above depend primarily

upon similarities of relation, for there is not much obvious similarity of property between, say, scales and feathers, taken apart from their relation to their respective organisms.

Another example illustrating this dual nature of analogy occurs in the *Topics*. The passage I am about to quote is a difficult and, I think, not wholly consistent one, since, as I shall argue later, Aristotle is here still in process of emancipating himself from a Platonic view of analogy that differs in several important respects from his own mature view. But part of this passage foreshadows his later understanding of the analogical relation:

> Likeness should be studied, first, in the case of things belonging to different genera, the formula being $A : B = C : D$ (e.g., as knowledge is to the object of knowledge, so sensation to the object of sensation), and as $A$ is in $B$, so is $C$ in $D$ (e.g., as sight is in the eye, so is reason in the soul, and as is a calm in the sea, so is windlessness in the air) (108 a).

We shall return to the first two examples in this passage later, but meanwhile we may note that "as is a calm in the sea, so is windlessness in the air" illustrates both senses of analogy distinguished above, for although these things are said here to belong to different genera, in the next section calmness in the sea and windlessness in the air are said to have in common that they are forms of rest, and hence to belong to the genus "rest." Thus what first looks like an analogy $A : B = C : D$ between different genera, becomes an analogy within a higher genus in virtue of the common form (rest) inhering in $A$ and $C$. This analogy depends both on the similarity of relation of calm to sea and windlessness to air, and on the form common to calm and windless. There would be no analogy without the common form, nor without the common relation. Thus, in his commentary on the *Posterior Analytics,* Ross seems to be mistaken when he interprets analogy without qualification as something between difference and specific identity, and adds "when the resemblance between two things is one of function or relation, not of inherent nature or structure" (8). If the analogous terms are within one genus, however high, their relation certainly lies between difference and *specific* identity, but is still in virtue of *some* identity of form between them and not only a resemblance of function or relation. Richard Robinson trivializes analogy in the same way when he remarks in a reply to a Thomist analysis that analogy in any sense other than mathematical proportionality "is merely the fact that some relations have more than one example" (9) and regards the assertion of an analogy $a$ is to $b$ as $c$ is to $d$ as merely equivalent to asserting the existence of an $R$ such that $aRb$ and $cRd$.

Aristotle does mention some examples, however, in which the analogy seems to rest almost entirely on the common relation in the second sense. Thus, he speaks in several places of the basic truths of logic and mathematics as being "one by analogy" when they apply in different fields, for example, in arithmetic, and geometry. Thus the axiom "take equals from equals and equals remain" is, he says, analogously common to arithmetic and geometry (*Post. An.* 76 a). Similarly the properties of proportionals in lines and in numbers are analogous: "Take the question why proportionals alternate. The cause when they are lines, and when they are numbers, is both different and identical; different in so far as lines are lines and not numbers, identical as involving a given determinate increment" (99 a). Now although identities and differences are involved here, this is not as in the first sense of analogy, for the identities are not between the terms taken separately but between the relations. That is to say, there is no property in common between the number 2 and a line *AB*, but there is a relation in common between 2 and 4 on the one hand, and the length *AB* and double its length on the other. Nothing is said about the individual terms other than that they are relata of a common relation. Furthermore, it is interesting to note that this is the only kind of analogy in which analogical *argument* is explicitly noticed by Aristotle; for since the proof of the properties of proportionals is the same for both analogues, this provides a justification for carrying the properties over from one to the other by analogy. Argument by analogy in the more modern sense of passing from known similarities between the properties of the analogues to further possible similarities is often used by Aristotle, but never explicitly discussed.

Aristotle's most interesting cases of scientific analogy occur in *De Sensu* and *De Anima,* and show that in his mature thought the analogy relation does usually combine senses one and two. Here he analyzes sensory qualities—colors, sounds, odors, flavors and tactile sensations—in terms of an ordering on a numerical scale. He regards compound colors and flavors as generated by intermediate ratios of extremes: white to black in the case of colors, sweet and bitter in the case of flavors. Thus they are "analogous to the sounds that enter into music" (439 b), and he supposes that, as with concords in music, simple ratios generate the most agreeable colors or flavors (an argument from analogy in the modern sense). But so far there is little more than analogy in sense two—likeness of relations on a numerical scale. Colors and flavors can be put into one to one relation to each other, as in lists abstracted by Ross (10), going from white via yellow, green, blue, purple, crimson, grey to black on the one hand, and from sweet via oily, harsh, pungent, astringent, acid, saline to bitter on the other. But there is no noticeable crosswise similarity between, for example, yellow and oily, blue and pungent, grey and saline, and so forth.

There is, however, more to be said. There are also analogies in sense one in these relations. There are analogies between odors and savors, in some cases, says Aristotle,. registered in language, "for odors as well as savors are spoken of as pungent, sweet, harsh, astringent, rich [= savory]" (443 b). Also in Greek there are metaphors from touch to sound in the equivalent of sharp and flat in music, and there are the real similarities of effects produced on the several sense organs by excess of sensory qualities or by pleasant or unpleasant combinations of them.[3]

Finally, there is a remarkable example that comes very close to the analogies appealed to in more modern scientific theories. In *Posterior Analytics* (98 a) Aristotle gives an example of a generic cause that is common to specifically different events, namely repercussion, which is common to echoes, reflections, and the rainbow. In *De Anima* (419 b) echoes are said to be masses of air rebounding like a ball from a wall, and "what happens here must be analogous to what happens in the case of light" when it is reflected. Now here we have both senses one and two of analogy—both the common features of situations: ball bouncing, echo, reflection, giving the form or generic cause "repercussion," and also the likeness of

3. "Acute and grave are here metaphors, transferred from their proper sphere, viz. that of touch, where they mean respectively (a) what moves the sense much in a short time, (b) what moves the sense little in a long time. . . . There seems to be a sort of parallelism between what is acute or grave to hearing and what is sharp or blunt to touch; what is sharp as it were stabs, while what is blunt pushes, the one producing its effect in a short, the other in a long time, so that the one is quick, the other slow" (*De Anima*, 420a).

relation in the causal chain of events connected with sound, light, and bouncing balls, namely, throwing, impact, and rebounding. This example illustrates well what Nagel (11) has called, in relation to modern theories, the *formal* and *substantive* analogies exhibited by scientific models, corresponding respectively with Aristotle's analogies two and one. Both kinds of analogy, as I have argued elsewhere, are necessary for the functioning of models as interpretations of scientific theories, both for purposes of *predicting* new properties by analogy, and of introducing *new theoretical terms* in an intelligible manner as extensions of scientific language.[4]

## METAPHYSICAL ANALOGY

There are two ways in which scientific analogy in Aristotle's sense might be said to be trivial. The first we have already noted. It consists in eliminating sense one, substantive analogy or the possession of common properties, and idenitfying the analogy relation with sense two, formal analogy or similarity of relation. However, it might seem that even substantive analogy in Aristotle's scientific examples is trivial, in that it depends on identical common prop-

---

4. Given part of the analogy between bouncing balls, sound, and light, as in Aristotle's example, it might be exploited in two ways: (a) to predict hitherto unknown properties of reflection, by analogy with echoes; (b) to "give meaning to" the theoretical term "light corpuscle," by analogy with "elastic ball."

For a development of this analysis of scientific models and meaning-relations see my paper, "On Defining Analogy," *Proc. Ar. Soc.,* LX (1959–60), 79.

erties, each of which is *univocally* predicated of its subject. But analogy proper, it may be argued, is *not* reducible to identities and differences: it is rather a third way between univocity and equivocity, and as such it does not really seem to be required in the scientific cases. It is this view that leads most of Aristotle's successors to neglect his scientific and concentrate upon his metaphysical analogies. What I shall call Aristotle's metaphysical examples occur precisely where the reduction to univocity or equivocity is impossible, and the third way seems to be demanded.

Before considering those metaphysical analogies that are typically Aristotelian, we should perhaps look briefly at some examples that should rather be called Platonic. In a passage from the *Topics* I have already quoted, Aristotle says that "likeness should be studied first in the case of things belonging to different genera, the formula being $A : B = C : D$," and gives as examples "as knowledge to the object of knowledge, so sensation to the object of sensation," and "as sight is in the eye, so is reason in the soul." These examples are Platonic in presupposing the division between the visible and intelligible worlds, and they certainly would fit very oddly into Aristotle's definition of analogy in terms of the classification system. In terms of this we should have to understand them in the sense that sight and reason, for example, are genera having certain common properties that place both in a higher genus, and this is certainly not what Plato understands by his analogies between levels of being. Aristotle does not in fact try to explain in this passage what the common properties are, as he does in the other example in the same passage, calm sea and windless air.

What is most obvious about the Platonic analogies is not the common properties of the terms, but the *relations* between sight and eye on the one hand and reason and soul on the other, and this seems to make the examples more like *formal* analogy (sense two) —as if we said "lines are to squares as numbers to square numbers" or spoke of equal ratios between pairs of rational and irrational numbers, without implying commensurability of individual terms. And, according to the usual interpretation, this *is* all that is intended in Plato's own discussion of these analogies. For example, in *Republic* (508 ff) the analogy between the *good* causing *knowledge* by *illuminating* the *soul,* and the *sun* causing *visual perception* by *lighting* the *eye,* is not actually taken to imply any direct similarity between the good and the sun, knowledge and perception, and so on, indeed the analogy is not supposed to say anything about the realm of the good, except in terms of its causal relations with visible things, and even what is meant here by "cause" remains obscure.

Aristotle's paradigm cases of analogy are derived from classifications rather than from incommensurable orders of being. But his discussion of the analogical character of the "good" leaves room neither for Plato's formal analogues of the Idea of the Good nor for his own analogy depending on common properties. "The Good is not some common element answering to one Idea. Goods are one by analogy" (*Ethics* 1096 b). So the problem, referred from the *Ethics* to the *Metaphysics,* is "How are things one by analogy, when there is no common element such as served to define the analogy-relation in the scientific classification cases?"

There are several references to analogy in *Metaphysics* that are hardly more than statements of this problem. In the discussion of "one" and "many" in Δ (1016 b) Aristotle says:

> Some things are one in number (whose matter is one) some in species (whose definition is one) some in genus (to which the same "figure of predication" applies), others by analogy (which are related as a third thing to a fourth).

"The same figure of predication" apparently means "the same category," and refers to Aristotle's belief implied elsewhere that the categories are the only true genera. Thus analogy is called in here precisely where its previous definition breaks down; that is, not to *define* a higher genus, but where there *is no higher genus,* as in the case of analogies across the categories. His gloss "are related as a third thing to a fourth" does not, because of the ambiguity about formal and substantive analogy, take us much further in understanding the nature of this relation.

The important cases of analogical relations across categories concern the metaphysical transcendentals: being, unity, goodness, actuality and potentiality, matter and form. Aristotle gives two kinds of examples to elucidate his meaning. The first is the well-known example of the predicate "healthy," as used properly of the state of health, and analogously and derivatively of medicine or exercise as the causes of health, a ruddy complexion as the effect of health, and so on. On this model we are to understand "being" used as a predicate in every category, and of all differentiae as well as all genera. Since no genus is predicated of its differentia, being cannot be itself a genus.

It is, however, predicated properly only of substance, and analogously and derivatively of the other categories. The comparison with "healthy" is perhaps unfortunate, because it directs attention to the *relations,* causal or otherwise, in virtue of which analogous predication of "healthy" is justified. But when being is predicated analogously of different categories, it is not relations of *this* kind between the categories which are in question. Properly speaking there are no such relations between categories, for relation is itself a category, and the being of a substance cannot "cause," or have any other relation to, the being of its attributes. The only sense in which anything like this could be said would itself be analogical, and thus would contribute nothing to the understanding of what it *is* to be analogical.

This difficulty affects all scholastic discussions of the "analogy of attribution," which depend on *causal* relations between the being of God and the being of creatures. Either the sense of "cause" here is univocal, in which case "healthy" but not "being" is a good paradigm for attributes of God and, worse, God is brought into the causal nexus of creatures, or else "cause" is itself analogical, in which case we are still in the dark about how attributes are predicated of God.

This is not the place to pursue the problem of the analogy of being as this was understood by Aristotle's successors. It may be suggested, however, that Aristotle's own intentions are shown more clearly in other, more neglected, examples. In *Metaphysics* Λ (1070 a), the elements form, privation, and matter, and the four causes, are said to be only analogically the same in different cases. White, black, and surface are form, privation, and matter, respectively, of color; . . . light, darkness, and air of day and night, but they are not so identically, but only in an analogical sense. The same thought is repeated in H (1042 b–43 a): the differentiae, in the sense of definitions, of sensible things, as for example, "ice is water frozen or solidified in such and such a way," have the same relation to the "matter," namely ice, that form, or actuality, or second substance, has to prime matter; that is to say, the differentiae in different special cases are *analogous* to second substance, to "what most resembles full actuality." Indeed it appears that we can only *know* substance, matter, form by the analogy of sensible things. The analogical process by which we learn the meaning of these and other metaphysical terms is made more explicit in a crucial passage in Θ (1048 a 35–b 8). Discussing the nature of actuality and potentiality, Aristotle says:

> What we mean can be plainly seen in the particular case by induction; we need not seek a definition for every term, but must grasp the analogy: that as that which is actually building is to that which is capable of building, so is that which is awake to that which is asleep; and that which is seeing to that which has the eyes shut, but has the power of sight; and that which is differentiated out of matter to the matter; and the finished article to the raw material. Let actuality be defined by one member of this antithesis, and the potential by the other.
>
> But things are not all said to exist actually in the same sense, but only by analogy—as $A$ is in $B$ or to $B$, so is $C$ in $D$ or to $D$; for the relation is either that of motion to potentiality, or that of substance to some particular matter.

Several points about this important passage require attention, in particular:

*First,* analogy is here, as before in the metaphysical examples, a method of definition that *replaces* that in terms of genus and differentiae when the definienda are not genera or species.

*Second,* the definition, or what here replaces the definition, is said to be given *by induction* from a number of examples that are here set out.

*Third,* the multiplication of examples enables us to "grasp the analogy" in a way reminiscent of the "grasp of the universal" which occurs according to Aristotle in every induction from a group of particulars.

*Fourth,* the resulting definienda do not however apply to the examples *in the same sense,* but only analogically.

Before attempting an analysis of this passage let us remind ourselves of the aims of this investigation. So far, Aristotle's use of scientific analogy has been shown to have essential features in common with that now current in the sciences; thus there is, as it were, an incentive to enquire into the relevance of his metaphysical analogy beyond the confines of his own philosophy. In particular, these metaphysical analogies seem to be primarily concerned with the *understanding* of metaphysical terms. Thus they are examples of the introduction of novel *language* by means of analogy, and this is equally a problem for modern scientific analogy, in the introduction of novel theoretical language.

The first impression given by Aristotle's attempt to "define" actuality and potentiality in the passage quoted is that either the nature of analogy must be assumed to be antecedently understood or there is an irreducible circle in the argument. We cannot understand what actuality is without grasping its analogical character, and yet what is meant by analogy is only (and perhaps *can* only be) indicated by Aristotle by exhibiting cases of definition by analogy similar to this one. Let us see, however, what clues are given by his reference to induction. Induction for Aristotle, as is well known, is a process of "grasping the universal" (*Post. An.* 81 b) through the perception of particulars. The process is, of course, closely akin to that by which species are elicited from individuals, and genera from species, by virtue of their common properties in the classification system. Again, therefore, analogy appears as the end term of a series of logical steps, applicable when the ordinary process of induction breaks down. For the induction referred to in this passage *Metaphysics* Θ is not the ordinary process of induction, though it may be related to it, because we are, as it were, invited to understand the "grasping of the analogy" *on the analogy of* the grasping of the universal by induction. What do the particular examples do to help us? Let us set them out in the form of proportionalities:

$$\frac{\text{building}}{\text{capable of building}} :: \frac{\text{awake}}{\text{asleep}} :: \frac{\text{seeing}}{\text{eyes shut}} :: \frac{\text{differentiated matter}}{\text{matter}}$$

$$:: \frac{\text{finished article}}{\text{raw material}} :: \quad \dots \quad = \frac{\text{ACTUALITY}}{\text{POTENTIALITY}} \quad [5]$$

5. The "analogy" between analogy and mathematical proportionality is of course limited. I have discussed this in the references given earlier in this chapter.

Induction takes place over the particular cases referred to by the pairs of terms. In each case our attention is directed to a *relation* between the terms. There is no reason why we should stop at these particular cases, indeed part of the process of grasping the analogy and coming to understand the actuality-potentiality relation is a coming to see that *every* particular exemplifies this relation. However, *mere* enumeration of the appropriate pair of terms in every particular would not constitute the relation, any more than mere enumeration of particulars constitutes a universal in the ordinary inductive case. So far the process has a good deal in common with induction of universals. It is, however, a *relation,* not a universal, that is grasped. And yet not only a relation, for actuality and potentiality are not indissolubly hyphenated in Aristotle's account. On the contrary, he claims that actuality and potentiality are defined by the sets of relata taken separately. Something more than a relation appears to be involved; in fact we have here something corresponding to the one-to-one similarities of substantive analogy. Building, waking, seeing, and so forth are not "actual" merely in virtue of being relata of a relation, say $R$, of which "actuality" is also a relatum; they are "actual" in virtue of themselves, just as particulars *are* particular cases of the universal. And yet "actuality" is not a universal, since it is not a member of the categorical classification, and, more important, it is not predicated of the particulars in the same sense but only analogically, whereas genus and species are always predicated literally (*Cat.* 3 a-b).

Thus we seem to be back in the definitional circle. The assistance given by comparison with induction breaks down exactly where we hoped it would throw light on the analogy relation itself as well as on the nature of the definition of these particular terms. Must we then be content to accept Aristotle's analogy as primitive and inexplicable? As far as Aristotle's own analysis goes this conclusion seems unavoidable. We are left with an analogical relation that, in the most significant cases, is not reducible to identities and differences and therefore has to be taken as an irreducible middle term between univocity and equivocity. We are, however, no nearer to understanding, except negatively, *what it is* for terms to be predicated analogically.

## UNIVOCITY AND ANALOGY

Let us now stand back from Aristotle's own discussion and attack the problem at a different point. Let us ask whether it is not in the concept of *univocity* rather than analogy that obscurity remains. Can the assumption be maintained that there are identities of properties in common between different particulars, and consequently that there are some names used univocally, as Aristotle asserts in Categories (1 a)? His whole account of the definition of species and genera, and of universals, of course presupposes the correctness of this assumption. There are admittedly hints in *Topics* that the "likenesses" between instances by means of which universals are brought in evidence may themselves be analogical (108 b, 160 a), but this suggestion receives no subsequent investigation in the Aristotelian corpus. And Aristotle's established position is seen not only in his discussion of analogy in *Metaphysics* but also in his discussion of metaphor in *Rhetoric* and *Poetics*. Some kinds of metaphor are there defined as depending on nonmetaphysical analogies: wherever there is a relation *B* is to *A* as *D* is to *C* we may metaphorically put *D* for *B,* and *B* for *D,* as in, for example, "sunset of life" for "old age." The metaphor has the same structure as scientific analogy and can also be used to coin new linguistic descriptions in novel situations by recognizing their similarity with old. But, says Aristotle, this use depends on the existence of nonmetaphoric descriptions; discourse cannot consist *wholly* of metaphor, for "a whole statement in such terms will be either a riddle or a barbarism" (*Poetics* 1458 a). In other words, metaphorical discourse is parasitic upon univocal and logically reducible to it.

In an extremely interesting paper entitled "Metaphor" (12), Max Black has contested this view. True metaphors, he there argues, depend neither upon the possibility of *substitution* of literal terms that exhaust the content of the metaphor, nor upon a purely external *comparison* between the metaphor and the original, where both are analyzed into identities and differences. Metaphors rather gain their force from *interaction* of the normal context of the metaphorical term with the context of the original, in a way that affects the meaning of *both*. To call a man a "wolf" is both to draw attention to certain aspects of a man which are called into mind by the associations of "wolf," and also, perhaps, reciprocally to affect the meaning of "wolf" in its original context, just as, for example, we can no longer use the word bestial in its original "literal" sense.

Such an interaction view opens up important possibilities. If it is correct, there need be no circularity in the view that, in a sense, all discourse *is* metaphorical, because the meanings of all words have long been affected by such interaction processes. Is there a parallel possibility that all predication is analogical? In other words that it is not that analogy is a queer and inexplicable hybrid, but rather that univocity is at best an oversimplification and at worst a highly misleading myth?

The first casualty of such a view would of course be Aristotle's account of induction.[6] In any case this would be generally regarded today as indefensible on other grounds, but there is no need to suppose that its demise carries into ruin all Aristotle's insights into analogy. Rather the contrary. In recognizing some cases of true analogy, Aristotle transcends his

6. Although not, interestingly enough, his examples quoted above of scientific analogies, which depend hardly at all on the existence of a fixed classification system defined univocally.

own presuppositions. And some of the difficulties inherent in his claim to knowledge of universals and of fixed species may be transformed by remarking that he has mistaken some cases of analogy for cases of identity. There is a certain looseness of fit at both ends of his definitional system, both with regard to the (unknowable) differences between particulars and with regard to the analogical relation between genera at the top. It would be more consistent to admit looseness of fit throughout. No two instances of a universal or of an inductive generalization are identical; neither is it clear that they can be analyzed explicitly into identities and differences, and even if they can, it seems that the same problem about the alleged identities will arise again. Hence, we are led to suggest every universal of inductive generalization is based on analogy between instances, and can be said to apply to those instances "in different senses," that is, analogously. There is of course something paradoxical in the view that, as Empson puts it, "you can only call a cat a cat by a metaphor" (13). And even if the ordinary notions of metaphor and analogy can be extended to cover cases where comparison with previous instances of similar things is involved, merely to point out that things are never named univocally only makes more urgent and does not ease the problem of explaining how things *are* named analogically.

   Two possible ways forward from this point may be suggested.

*First,* for practical and approximate purposes it may be sufficient to analyze similarities between instances by means of degrees of similarity shading from near-identity to near-total difference, relying perhaps on enumeration of similar or different characteristics in the related instances and deciding that a sufficient similarity can be taken as identity. This might be elaborated with as much formal complexity as required, as suggested, for example, by Wittgenstein's analysis of universals into family resemblances rather than into identities between instances (14, 15). *Second,* more fundamentally, we may take a hint from Black's analysis of metaphor. The relation between two things of which the same word is predicated is a symmetrical relation; the predication is metaphorical in *both* cases, not literal in one and metaphorical in the other, and this is so because of an *interaction* of meanings of the word in the two contexts. Similarities become highlighted and differences disregarded, and this in turn leads to further similarities being noted, whereas further differences will be overlooked. Imagine this process taking place between two individuals placed in the same species or two objects predicated by the same universal. The process is based initially on an observed similarity of things which tends to be highlighted by use of the same word in both cases. The meaning of the word adjusts itself to cope with the differences between the cases, and further differences in other cases judged sufficiently similar to come under the same species.

Sometimes the differences may be *unsayable,* because there has never been occasion to coin a word for them, as for instance between different shades of red. Meaning also adjusts itself to deal with what turn out to be convenient classifications when related to other classifications. But no equilibrium of meaning and classification is ever final, for there are any number of ways in which a classification may break down. For example, it is no longer the case that "atom" means "indivisible particle"; whales are not conveniently classified as fish; and on the other hand distinctions previously made are abandoned or possible distinctions never made, as in the (possible apocryphal) case of the Eskimo's twenty-seven different varieties of snow. Something like this seems to be what is involved in the difficult notion of a predicate not applying to its instances "in the same sense but analogically." Would not the Eskimo be inclined to say that the English "snow" is an analogical term? There is no clear sense in which the application of this word to his twenty-seven varieties could be reduced to identities and differences describable in English, and we should, for example, probably not attempt to *learn* the Eskimo language this way.

These suggestions require more elaboration than I have given them here. They are offered to indicate that a study of Aristotle's logic of analogy need not be merely antiquarian and that several problems that are closely connected in Aristotle's discussion would still benefit from being considered together, although not from the point of view of his own reliance on univocity as a primitive notion. How, if at all, this conclusion would ease the problem of metaphysical analogy is beyond the scope of this paper. In Aristotle's case, I think it would have little direct effect, since he in any case *presupposes* analogical predication in order to discuss the metaphysical terms. Its effect would rather be on his theory of induction and of science. But the conclusion should give no comfort at all to those neoscholastics and others who try to elucidate analogy in metaphysical and theological contexts from an Aristotelian standpoint. There are, I submit, *no* further resources in Aristotle for this undertaking, precisely because the elucidation of analogy was not his problem and because progress appears to depend on the rejection of his assumptions about univocity. He was right, however, in seeing a close link between the (for him) pseudo analogies of science and the true analogies of metaphysics, and this insight can be salvaged, indeed should be energetically exploited, because we now know far more than he could have known about the analogical uses of language implicit in the growth of science. The relevance of this to metaphysics and theology may not be negligible.

# The Explanatory Function
# of Metaphor [1]

The thesis of this paper is that the deductive model
of scientific explanation should be modified and supplemented by a view of theoretical explanation as
metaphoric redescription of the domain of the explanandum. This raises two large preliminary questions: first, whether the deductive model requires
modification, and second, what is the view of metaphor presupposed by the suggested alternative. I
shall not discuss the first question explicitly. Much
recent literature in the philosophy of science (for
example, 4, 5, 10, 14)[2] has answered it affirmatively,
and I shall refer briefly at the end to some difficulties
tending to show that a new model of explanation is
required, and suggest how the conception of theories
as metaphors meets these difficulties.

The second question, about the view of metaphor
presupposed, requires more extensive discussion.
The view I shall present is essentially due to Max
Black, who has developed in two papers, entitled,
respectively, "Metaphor" and "Models and Arche-
types" (3), both a new theory of metaphor and a

1. Presented at the Congress of the International Union for the Logic,
Methodology and Philosophy of Science, Jerusalem, March, 1964. Re-
printed by permission.
2. Numbers in parentheses refer to literature listed in the Bibliography at the end of this volume.

parallelism between the use of literary metaphor and the use of models in theoretical science. I shall start with an exposition of Black's *interaction view* of metaphors and models, taking account of modifications suggested by some of the subsequent literature on metaphor (1, 2, 11, 13, 15). It is still unfortunately necessary to argue that metaphor is more than a decorative literary device and that it has cognitive implications whose nature is a proper subject of philosophic discussion. But space forces me to mention these arguments as footnotes to Black's view, rather than as an explicit defence *ab initio* of the philosophic importance of metaphor.

## THE INTERACTION VIEW OF METAPHOR

1. We start with two systems, situations, or referents, which will be called, respectively, the "primary" and the "secondary" systems. Each is describable in literal language. A metaphoric use of language in describing the primary system consists of transferring to it a word or words normally used in connection with the secondary system: for example, "Man is a wolf," "Hell is a lake of ice." In a scientific theory the primary system is the domain of the explanandum, describable in observation language; the secondary is the system, described either in observation language or the language of a familiar theory, from which the model is taken: for example, "Sound (primary system) is propagated by wave motion (taken from a secondary system)"; "Gases are col-

lections of randomly moving massive particles."

Three terminological remarks should be inserted here. First, "primary system" and "secondary system" and "domain of the explanandum" will be used throughout to denote the referents or putative referents of descriptive statements; "metaphor," "model," "theory," "explanans," and "explanandum" will be used to denote linguistic entities. Second, use of the terms "metaphoric" and "literal," "theory" and "observation" need not be taken at this stage to imply a pair of irreducible dichotomies. All that is intended is that the literal and observation languages are assumed initially to be well understood and unproblematic, whereas the metaphoric and theoretical are in need of analysis. The third remark is that to assume initially that the two systems are "described" in literal or observation language does not imply that they are exhaustively or accurately described or even that they could in principle be so in terms of these languages.

2. We assume that the primary and secondary systems each carries a set of associated ideas and beliefs that come to mind when the system is referred to. These are not private to individual language-users but are largely common to a given language community and are presupposed by speakers who intend to be understood in that community. In literary contexts the associations may be loosely knit and variable, as in the wolf-like characteristics that come to mind when the metaphor "Man is a wolf" is used;

in scientific contexts the primary and secondary systems may both be highly organized by networks of natural laws.

A remark must be added here about the use of the word "meaning." Writers on metaphor appear to intend it as an inclusive term for reference, use, and the relevant set of associated ideas. It is, indeed, part of their thesis that it has to be understood thus widely. To understand the meaning of a descriptive expression is not only to be able to recognize its referent, or even to use the words in the expression correctly, but also to call to mind the ideas, both linguistic and empirical, that are commonly held to be associated with the referent in the given language community. Thus a shift of meaning may result from a change in the set of associated ideas as well as in change of reference or use.

3. For a conjunction of terms drawn from the primary and secondary systems to constitute a metaphor it is necessary that there should be patent falsehood or even absurdity in taking the conjunction literally. Man is not, literally, a wolf; gases are not in the usual sense collections of massive particles. In consequence some writers have denied that the referent of the metaphoric expression can be identified with the primary system without falling into absurdity or contradiction. I shall return to this in the next section.

4. There is initially some principle of assimilation between primary and secondary systems, vari-

ously described in the literature as "analogy," "intimations of similarity," "a programme for exploration," "a framework through which the primary is seen." Here we have to guard against two opposite interpretations, both of which are inadequate for the general understanding of metaphors and scientific models. On the one hand, to describe this ground of assimilation as a *program* for exploration or a *framework* through which the primary is seen, is to suggest that the secondary system can be imposed a priori upon the primary, as if *any* secondary can be the source of metaphors or models for *any* primary, provided the right metaphor-creating operations are subsequently carried out. Black does indeed suggest that in some cases "it would be more illuminating . . . to say that the metaphor creates the similarity than to say it formulates some similarity antecedently existing" (p. 37), and he also points out that some poetry creates new metaphors precisely by developing itself the system of associations in terms of which "absurd" conjunctions of words are to be metaphorically understood.

There is, however, an important distinction to be brought out between such a use of metaphor and scientific models, for, whatever may be the case for poetic use, the suggestion that *any* scientific model can be imposed a priori on *any* explanandum and function fruitfully in its explanation must be resisted. Such a view would imply that theoretical models are irrefutable. That this is not the case is sufficiently illustrated by the history of the concept of a heat fluid or the classical wave theory of light. Such examples also indicate that no model even gets off the ground unless some antecedent similarity or analogy is discerned between it and the explanandum.

But here there is a danger of falling into what Black calls the *comparison view* of metaphor. According to this view the metaphor can be replaced without remainder by an explicit, literal statement of the similarities between primary and secondary systems, in other words, by a simile. Thus, the metaphor "Man is a wolf" would be equivalent to "Man is like a wolf in that . . ." where follows a list of comparable characteristics; or, in the case of theoretical models, the language derived from the secondary system would be wholly replaced by an explicit statement of the analogy between secondary and primary systems, after which further reference to the secondary system would be dispensable. Any interesting examples of model-using in science will show, however, that the situation cannot be described in this way. For one thing, as long as the model is under active consideration as an ingredient in an explanation, we do not know how far the comparison extends—it is precisely in its extension that the fruitfulness of the model may lie. And a more fundamental objection to the comparison view emerges in considering the next point.

5. The metaphor works by transferring the asso-

ciated ideas and implications of the secondary to the primary system. These select, emphasize, or suppress features of the primary; new slants on the primary are illuminated; the primary is "seen through" the frame of the secondary. In accordance with the doctrine that even literal expressions are understood partly in terms of the set of associated ideas carried by the system they describe, it follows that the associated ideas of the primary are changed to some extent by the use of the metaphor and that, therefore, even its original literal description is shifted in meaning. The same applies to the secondary system, for its associations come to be affected by assimilation to the primary; the two systems are seen as more like each other; they seem to interact and adapt to one another, even to the point of invalidating their original literal descriptions if these are understood in the new, postmetaphoric sense. Men are seen to be more like wolves after the wolf metaphor is used, and wolves seem to be more human. Nature becomes more like a machine in the mechanical philosophy, and actual, concrete machines themselves are seen as if stripped down to their essential qualities of mass in motion.

This point is the kernel of the interaction view and is Black's major contribution to the analysis of metaphor. It is incompatible with the comparison view, which assumes that the literal descriptions of both systems are and remain independent of the use of the metaphor and that the metaphor is reducible to them. The consequences of the interaction view for theoretical models are also incompatible with assumptions generally made in the deductive account of explanation, namely, that descriptions and descriptive laws in the domain of the explanandum remain empirically acceptable and invariant in meaning to all changes of explanatory theory. I shall return to this point.

6. It should be added as a final point in this preliminary analysis that a metaphoric expression used for the first time, or used to someone who hears it for the first time, is intended to be *understood*. Indeed, it may be said that a metaphor is not metaphor but nonsense if it communicates nothing and that a genuine metaphor is also capable of communicating something other than was intended and hence of being *mis*understood. If I say (taking two words more or less at random from a dictionary page) "A truck is a trumpet," it is unlikely that I shall communicate anything; if I say "He is a shadow on the weary land," you may understand me to mean (roughly) "He is a wet blanket, a gloom, a menace," whereas I actually meant (again roughly) "He is a shade from the heat, a comfort, a protection."

Acceptance of the view that metaphors are meant to be intelligible implies rejection of all views that make metaphor a wholly noncognitive, subjective, emotive, or stylistic use of language. There are exactly parallel views of scientific models that have been held by many contemporary philosophers of science, namely, that models are purely subjective, psychological, and adopted by individuals for private heuristic purposes. But this is wholly to misdescribe their function in science. Models, like metaphors, are intended to communicate. If some theorist develops a theory in terms of a model, he does not regard it as a private language but presents it as an ingredient of his theory. Neither can he, nor need he, make literally explicit all the associations of the model he is exploiting; other workers in the field "catch on" to its intended implications— indeed, they sometimes find the theory unsatisfactory just because some implications the model's originator did not investigate, or even think of, turn out to be empirically false. None of this would be possible unless use of the model were intersubjective, part of the commonly understood theoretical language of science, not a private language of the individual theorist.

An important general consequence of the interaction view is that it is not possible to make a distinction between literal and metaphoric descriptions merely by asserting that literal use consists in following linguistic rules. Intelligible metaphor also implies the existence of rules of metaphoric use, and since in the interaction view literal meanings are shifted by their association with metaphors, it follows that the rules of literal usage and of metaphor, though they are not identical, are nevertheless not independent. It is not sufficiently clear in Black's paper that the interaction view commits one to the abandonment of a two-tiered account of language in which some usages are irreducibly literal and others metaphoric. The interaction view sees language as dynamic: an expression initially metaphoric may become literal (a "dead" metaphor), and what is at one time literal may become metaphoric (for example, the Homeric "He breathed forth his life," originally literal, is now a metaphor for death). What is important is not to try to draw a line between the methaphoric and the literal, but rather to trace out the various mechanisms of meaning-shift and their interactions. The interaction view cannot consistently be made to rest on an initial set of absolutely literal descriptions, but rather on a relative distinction of literal and metaphoric in particular contexts. I cannot undertake the task of elucidating these conceptions here (an interesting attempt to do so has been made by K. I. B. S. Needham (12), but I shall later point out a parallel between this general linguistic situation and the relative distinctions and mutual interactions of theory and observation in science.

### THE PROBLEM OF METAPHORIC REFERENCE

One of the main problems for the interaction view in its application to theoretical explanation is the question what is the *referent* of a model or metaphor. At first sight the referent seems to be the primary system, which we choose to describe in metaphoric rather than literal terms. This, I believe, is in the end the right answer, but the process of metaphoric description is such as to cast doubt on any simple identification of the metaphor's reference with the primary system. It is claimed in the interaction view that a metaphor causes us to "see" the primary system differently and causes the meanings of terms originally literal in the primary system to shift toward the metaphor. Thus "Man is a wolf" makes man seem more vulpine, "Hell is a lake of ice" makes hell seem icy rather than hot, and a wave theory of sound makes sound seem more vibrant. But how can initial similarities between the objective systems justify such changes in the meanings of words and even, apparently, in the things themselves? Man does not in fact change because someone uses the wolf metaphor. How then can we be justified in identifying what we see through the framework of the metaphor with the primary system itself? It seems that we cannot be entitled to say that men *are* wolves, sound *is* wave motion, in any identificatory sense of the copula.

Some recent writers on metaphor (2, 11, 15) have made it the main burden of their argument to deny that any such identification is possible. They argue that if we allow it we are falling into the absurdity of conjoining two literally incompatible systems, and the resulting expression is not metaphoric but meaningless. By thus taking a metaphor literally we turn it into a myth. An initial misunderstanding may be removed at once by remarking that "identification" cannot mean in this context identification of the referent of the metaphoric expression, taken in its *literal* sense, with the primary system. But if the foregoing analysis of metaphor is accepted, it follows that metaphoric use is use different from the literal sense, and furthermore it is use in a sense not replaceable by any literal expression. There remains the question what it is to identify the referent of the metaphoric expression or model with the primary system.

As a preliminary to answering this question, it is important to point out that there are two ways, which are often confused in accounts of the "meaning of theoretical concepts," in which such identification may fail. It may fail because it is in principle meaningless to make any such identification, or it may fail because in a particular case the identification happens to be false. Instances of false identification, e.g., "Heat is a fluid" or "The substance emitted by a burning object is phlogiston," provide no arguments to show that other such identifications may not be both meaningful and true.

Two sorts of argument have been brought against the view that metaphoric expressions and models can refer to and truly describe the primary system. The first depends on an assimilation of poetic and scientific metaphor and points out that it is characteristic of good poetic metaphor that the images introduced are initially striking and unexpected, if not shocking; that they are meant to be entertained and savored for the moment and not analyzed in pedantic detail nor stretched to radically new situations; and that they may immediately give place to other metaphors referring to the same subject matter which are formally contradictory, and in which the contradictions are an essential part of the total metaphoric impact. Any attempt to separate these literal contradictions from the nexus of interactions is destructive of the metaphor, particularly in the interaction view. In the light of these characteristics there is indeed a difficult problem about the correct analysis of the notion of metaphoric "truth" in poetic contexts. Scientific models, however, are fortunately not so intractable. They do not share any of the characteristics listed above that make poetic metaphors peculiarly subject to formal contradictoriness. They may initially be unexpected, but it is not their chief aim to shock; they are meant to be exploited energetically and often in extreme quantitative detail and in quite novel observational domains; they are meant to be internally tightly knit by logical and causal interrelations; and if two models of the same primary system are found to be mutually inconsistent, this is not taken (*pace* the complementarity interpretation of quantum physics) to enhance their effectiveness but rather as a challenge to reconcile them by mutual modification or to refute one of them. Thus their truth criteria, although not rigorously formalizable, are at least much clearer than in the case of poetic metaphor. We can perhaps signalize the difference by speaking in the case of scientific models of the (perhaps unattainable) aim to find a "perfect metaphor," whose referent is the domain of the explanandum, whereas literary metaphors, however adequate and successful in their own terms, are from the point of view of potential logical consistency and extendability often (not always) intentionally imperfect.

Second, if the interaction view of scientific metaphor or model is combined with the claim that the referent of the metaphor is the primary system (that is, the metaphor is true of the primary system), then it follows that the thesis of meaning-invariance of the literal observation-descriptions of the primary system is false. For, the interaction view implies that the meaning of the original literal language of the primary system is changed by adoption of the metaphor. Hence those who wish to adhere to meaning-invariance in the deductive account of explanation will be forced to reject either the interaction view or the realistic view that a scientific model is putatively true of its primary system. Generally they reject both. But abandonment of meaning-invariance, as in many recent criticisms of the deductive model of explanation, leaves room for adoption of both the interaction view and realism, as I shall now try to spell out in more detail.

## EXPLANATION AS METAPHORIC REDESCRIPTION

The initial contention of this paper was that the deductive model of explanation should be *modified* and *supplemented* by a view of theoretical explanation as metaphoric redescription of the domain of the explanandum. First, the association of the ideas of metaphor and of explanation requires more examination. It is certainly not the case that all explanations are metaphoric. To take only two examples, explanation by covering-law, where an instance of *A* which is *B* is explained by reference to the law "All *A's* are *B's*" is not metaphoric; neither is the explanation of the working of a mechanical gadget by reference to an actual mechanism of cogs, pulleys, and levers. These, however, are not examples of *theoretical* explanation, for it has been taken for granted that the essence of a theoretical explanation is the introduction into the explanans of a new vocabulary or even of a new language. But introduction of a metaphoric terminology is not in itself explanatory, for in literary metaphor in general there is no hint that what is metaphorically described is also thereby explained. The connection between metaphor and explanation is, therefore, neither that of necessary nor sufficient condition. Metaphor becomes explanatory only when it satisfies certain further conditions.

The orthodox deductive criteria for a scientific explanans—for example, in Hempel and Oppenheim (6)—require that the explanandum be deducible from it, that it contain at least one general law not redundant to the deduction, that it be not empirically falsified to date, and that it be predictive. We cannot simply graft these requirements on to the account of theories as metaphors without investigating the consequences of the interaction view of metaphor for the notions of "deducibility," "explanandum," and "falsification" in the orthodox account. In any case, as has been mentioned already, the requirement of deducibility in particular has been subjected to damaging attack, quite apart from any metaphoric interpretation of theories. There are two chief grounds for this attack, both of which can be turned into arguments favorable to the metaphoric view.

In the first place, it is pointed out that there is seldom in fact a deductive relation strictly speaking between scientific explanans and explanandum, but only relations of approximate fit. Furthermore, what counts as sufficiently approximate fit cannot be decided deductively but is a complicated function of coherence with the rest of a theoretical system, general empirical acceptability throughout the domain of the explanandum, and many other factors. I do not propose to try to spell out these relationships in further detail here, but merely to make two points relevant to my immediate concern. First, the attack on deducibility drawn from the occurrence of approximations does not imply that there are *no* deductive relations between explanans and explanandum. The situation is rather this. Given a descriptive statement $D$ in the domain of the explanandum, it is usually the case that the statement $E$ of an acceptable explanans does not entail $D$, but rather $D'$, where $D'$ is a statement in the domain of the explanandum only "approximately equivalent" to $D$. For $E$ to be acceptable it is necessary both that there be a deductive relation between $E$ and $D'$, and that $D'$ should come to be recognized as a *more acceptable* description in the domain of the explanandum than $D$. The reasons why it might be more acceptable—repetition of the experiments with greater accuracy, greater coherence with other acceptable laws, recognition of disturbing factors in arriving at $D$ in the first place, metaphoric shifts in the meanings of terms in $D$ consequent upon the introduction of the new terminology of $E$, and so on—need not concern us here. What is relevant is that the nondeducibility of $D$ from $E$ does not imply total abandonment of the deductive model unless $D$ is regarded as an invariant description of the explanandum, automatically rendering $D'$ empirically false. That $D$ cannot be so regarded has been amply demonstrated in the literature.

The second point of contact between these considerations and the view of theories as metaphors is now obvious. That explanation may modify and correct the explanandum is already built into the relation between metaphors and the primary system in the interaction view. Metaphors, if they are good ones, and ipso facto their deductive consequences, do have the primary system as their referents, for they may be seen as correcting and replacing the original literal descriptions of the same system, so that the literal descriptions are discarded as inadequate or even false. The parallel with the deductive relations of explanans and explananda is clear: the metaphoric view does not abandon deduction, but it focusses attention rather on the interaction between metaphor and primary system, and on the criteria of acceptability of metaphoric descriptions of the primary system, and hence not so much upon the deductive relations that appear in this account as comparatively uninteresting pieces of logical machinery.

The second attack upon the orthodox deductive account gives even stronger and more immediate grounds for the introduction of the metaphoric view. It is objected that there are no deductive relations between theoretical explanans and explanandum because of the intervention of correspondence rules. If the deductive account is developed, as it usually is, in terms either of an uninterpreted calculus and an observation language, or of two distinct languages —the theoretical and the observational, it follows that the correspondence rules linking terms in these languages cannot be derived deductively from the explanans alone. Well-known problems then arise about the status of the correspondence rules and about the meaning of the predicates of the theoretical language. In the metaphoric view, however, these problems are evaded, because here there are no correspondence rules, and this view is primarily designed to give its own account of the meaning of the language of the explanans. There is *one* language, the observation language, which like all natural languages is continually being extended by metaphoric uses and hence yields the terminology of the explanans. There is no problem about connecting explanans and explanadum other than the general problem of understanding how metaphors are introduced and applied and exploited in their primary systems. Admittedly, as yet we are far from understanding this process, but to see the problem of the "meaning of theoretical concepts" as a special case of it is one step in the solution of this problem.

Finally, a word about the requirement that an explanation be predictive. It has been much debated within the orthodox deductive view whether this is a necessary and sufficient condition for explanation, and it is not appropriate here to enter into that debate. But any account of explanation would be inadequate which did not recognize that, in general, an explanation is required to be predictive or, what is closely connected with this, to be falsifiable. Elsewhere (8) I have pointed out that, in terms of the deductive view, the requirement of predictivity may mean one of three things.

1. That general laws already present in the explanans have as yet unobserved instances. This is a trivial fulfilment of the requirement and would not, I think, generally be regarded as sufficient.

2. That further general laws can be derived from the explanans *without* adding further items to the set of correspondence rules. That is to say, predictions remain within the domain of the set of predicates already present in the explanandum. This is a weak sense of predictivity that covers what would normally be called *applications* rather than extensions of a theory (for example, calculation of the orbit of a satellite from the theory of gravitation but not extension of the theory to predict the bending of light rays).

3. There is also a strong sense of prediction in which new observation predicates are involved, and hence, in terms of the deductive view, additions are required to the set of correspondence rules. I have argued (7, 8) that there is no rational method of adding to the correspondence rules on the pure deductive view, and hence that cases of strong prediction cannot be rationally accounted for on that view. In the metaphoric view, on the other hand, since the domain of the explanandum is redescribed in terminology transferred from the secondary system, it is to be expected that the original observation language will both be shifted in meaning and extended in vocabulary, and hence that predictions in the strong sense will become possible. They may, of course, turn out not to be *true,* but that is an occupational hazard of any explanation or prediction. They will, however, be rational, because rationality consists just in the continuous adaptation of

our language to our continually expanding world, and metaphor is one of the chief means by which this is accomplished.

# Bibliography

The *loci classici* of the dispute about models are:

Duhem, P., *The Aim and Structure of Physical Theory* (Princeton: 1954), Part I, Chapter IV. (First published as *La Théorie physique,* Paris, 1914.)

Campbell, N. R., *Physics, the Elements* (Cambridge: 1920), Chapter VI. (Now in Dover edition entitled *Foundations of Science.*)

*THE FUNCTION OF MODELS: A DIALOGUE*
More recent general discussion of the topics of this chapter will be found in:

Barker, S. F., *Induction and Hypothesis* (Ithaca, N. Y.: 1957).

Black, M., *Models and Metaphors* (Ithaca, N. Y.: 1962), Chapters 3 and 13.

Braithwaite, R. B., *Scientific Explanation* (Cambridge: 1953), Chapter IV.

————"Models in the Empirical Sciences," in Nagel, E., *et al.,* eds., *Proceedings of the Congress of the International Union for the Logic, Methodology and Philosophy of Science* (Stanford: 1960).

Hanson, N. R., *Patterns of Discovery* (Cambridge: 1958).

Harre, H. R., *Theories and Things,* Newman History and Philosophy of Science Series (London: 1961).

Hempel, C. G., and Oppenheim, P., "The Logic of Explanation," in Feigl, H., and Brodbeck, M., eds., *Readings in the Philosophy of Science* (New York: 1953), p. 319.

Hesse, Mary B., "Models in Physics," *B.J.P.S.,* IV (1953), 198.

———— *Forces and Fields* (London: 1961), Chapter I.

Hutten, E. H., "On Semantics and Physics," *Proc. Aris. Soc.,* XLIX (1948–9), 115.

————"The Role of Models in Physics," *B.J.P.S.,* IV (1953), 284.

————*The Language of Modern Physics* (London: 1956), Chapters V and VI.

Nagel, E., *The Structure of Science* (London: 1961), Chapters V and VI.

Various types of models are discussed from the biological point of view in:

Beament, J. W. L., ed., *Models and Analogues in Biology,* Symposium of the Society for Experimental Biology (Cambridge: 1960).

And from the logical point of view in:

Freudenthal, H., ed., *The Concept and the Role of the Model in Mathematics and Natural and Social Science* (Dordrecht: 1961).

Feyerabend, P. K., "An Attempt at a Realistic Interpretation of Experience," *Proc. Aris. Soc.,* LVIII (1957–8), 143.

————"Complementarity," Aristotelian Society Supplementary Volume, XXXII (1958), 75.

Aristotle's discussions of the analogies between the objects of the various senses are in *De Anima,* 419–426, and *De Sensu,* 438–43.

## MATERIAL ANALOGY

There is some discussion of analogical reasoning in most of the standard works on logic and scientific method, for example:

Mill, J. S., *System of Logic,* Book III, Chapter XX.

Jevons, W. S., *Principles of Science,* Chapter XXVIII.

Johnson, W. E., *Logic,* I, Chapter XIII, §3; III, Chapter IV.

Stebbing, L. S., *Modern Introduction to Logic,* Chapter XIV, §3.

Cohen, M. R., and Nagel, E., *Logic and Scientific Method,* pp. 286 ff.

Russell, B., *Human Knowledge, Its Scope and Limits,* Part VI, Chapter VIII.

Hospers, J., *Introduction to Philosophical Analysis,* pp. 353 ff., 371 ff.

More detailed development of the formal properties of the four-term analogy relation will be found in:

Hesse, Mary B., "On Defining Analogy," *Proc. Aris. Soc.,* LX (1959–60), 79.

## THE LOGIC OF ANALOGY

Standard texts on confirmation theory are:

Keynes, J. M., *A Treatise on Probability* (London:

1921), especially Chapters XVIII and XIX on analogical argument.

Broad, C. D., "Problematic Induction," *Proc. Aris. Soc.* (1927–8), p. 1.

Carnap, R., *Logical Foundations of Probability* (London: 1950).

For a criticism of confirmation theory and further development of the logics of analogy see:

Wright, G. H. von, *The Logical Problem of Induction,* 2nd ed. (Oxford: 1957), especially Chapter VI.

The impossibility of justifying analogical argument in a "chance" universe is pointed out in:

Hosiasson, J. L., "Induction et Analogie: comparaison de leur fondement," *Mind,* 50 (1941), 351.

Popper's own account of his falsifiability criterion is best read in:

Popper, K. R., *The Logic of Scientific Discovery* (London: 1959).

The best recent general discussion of simplicity as a criterion for theories is:

"Discussion on Simplicity," articles by R. S. Rudner, M. Bunge, N. Goodman, and R. Ackermann, *Philosophy of Science,* 28, (1961), 109.

## THE EXPLANATORY FUNCTION OF METAPHOR

1. Beardsley, M. C., *Aesthetics* (New York: 1958).

2. Berggren, D., "The Use and Abuse of Metaphor," *Rev. Met.,* XVI (1962), 237, 450.

3. Black, M., *Models and Metaphors* (Ithaca, N. Y.: 1962).

4. Feyerabend, P. K., "An Attempt at a Realistic Interpretation of Experience," *Proc. Aris. Soc.,* LVIII (1957), 143.

5. _____"Explanation, Reduction and Empiricism," in Feigl, H., and Maxwell, G., eds., *Minnesota Studies* III (1963).

6. Hempel, C. G., and Oppenheim, P., "The Logic of Explanation," in Feigl, H., and Brodbeck, M., eds., *Readings in the Philosophy of Science* (New York: 1953), p. 319.

7. Hesse, Mary B., "Theories, Dictionaries and Observations," *Brit. J. Phil. Sc.,* IX (1958), 12, 128.

8. _____*Models and Analogies in Science* (London: Sheed and Ward, 1953).

9. _____"A New Look at Scientific Explanation," *Rev. Met.,* XVII (1963), 198.

10. Kuhn, T. S., *The Structure of Scientific Revolutions* (Chicago: 1962).

11. McCloskey, Mary A., "Metaphors," *Mind,* LXXIII (1964), 215.

12. Needham, K. I. B. S., "Synonymy and Semantic Classification," Cambridge Ph.D. dissertation, 1964.

13. Schon, D., *The Displacement of Concepts* (London: 1963).

14. Sellars, W., "The Language of Theories," in Feigl, H., and Maxwell, G., eds., *Current Issues in the Philosophy of Science* (New York: 1961).

15. Turbayne, C., *The Myth of Metaphor* (New Haven: 1962).

## ARISTOTLE'S THEORY OF ANALOGY

Out of the enormous literature related more or less directly to Thomist analogy, I have made the following highly subjective selection:

1. Garrigou-Lagrange, R., *God, His Existence and His Nature* (in translation) (London: 1934).

2. Penido, R. T.-L., *Le Rôle de l'Analogie en Théologie Dogmatique* (Paris: 1931).

3. Bochenski, T. M., "On Analogy," *The Thomist,* XI (1948), 424, and the review by R. Feys, *Journal of Symbolic Logic,* 14 (1949), 265.

4. Lyttkens, H., *The Analogy Between God and the World* (Uppsala: 1952).

5. Ross, James F., "Analogy as a Rule of Meaning for Religious Language," *Int. Phil. Quart.,* I (1961), 468.

6. Weiter, G., "Beliefs and Attributes," *Philosophy* 36 (1961), 196.

And on analogy in Greek philosophy:

7. Lloyd, G. E. R., "Two Types of Argumentation in Early Greek Thought," Cambridge Ph.D. dissertation, 1958.

8. Ross, W. D., *Aristotle's Prior and Posterior Analytics* (Oxford: 1949), p. 670.

9. Robinson, R., *Review of Metaphysics,* V (1952), 466.

10. Ross, J. F., *Aristotle Parva Naturalia* (Oxford: 1955), p. 206.

11. Nagel, E., *The Structure of Science* (London: 1961), p. 110.

12. Black, M., *Models and Metaphors* (Ithaca, N. Y.: 1962), p. 25.

13. Empson, W., *The Structure of Complex Words* (London: 1951), p. 331.

14. Wittgenstein, L., *Philosophical Investigations* §67.

15. Bambrough, R., "Universals and Family Resemblances," *Proc. Aris. Soc.* LXI (1960–61), 207.